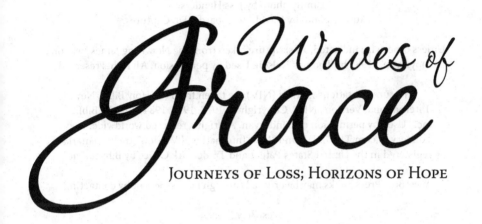

Waves of Grace

Journeys of Loss; Horizons of Hope

Meredith Shave

WESTBOW
PRESS®
A DIVISION OF THOMAS NELSON
& ZONDERVAN

Family photo by Jess Henderson.
Author photo by David Longobardo, DL Captures.

Unless otherwise indicated, all scripture taken from the New King James Version®. Copyright © 1982 by Thomas Nelson. Used by permission. All rights reserved.

Scripture quotations marked (NIV) are taken from the Holy Bible, New International Version®, NIV®. Copyright © 1973, 1978, 1984, 2011 by Biblica, Inc.™ Used by permission of Zondervan. All rights reserved worldwide. www.zondervan.com The "NIV" and "New International Version" are trademarks registered in the United States Patent and Trademark Office by Biblica, Inc.™

WestBow Press books may be ordered through booksellers or by contacting:

WestBow Press
A Division of Thomas Nelson & Zondervan
1663 Liberty Drive
Bloomington, IN 47403
www.westbowpress.com
1 (866) 928-1240

ISBN: 978-1-9736-4232-9 (sc)
ISBN: 978-1-9736-4231-2 (hc)
ISBN: 978-1-9736-4233-6 (e)

Library of Congress Control Number: 2018912059

Print information available on the last page.

WestBow Press rev. date: 10/25/2018

To Jon ...

Kind-hearted and selfless, you have become my favorite person and very best friend. You, my darling, take "saving the best for last" to a whole new level. Encouraging me to share my past to give others hope is just one of the many reasons I love you.

Together forever,
Mer

Contents

The Empty Chair

The picture for the cover of this book revealed itself as I searched through hundreds of my sunrise photos. I kept going back to the ones of the aged Adirondack chair.

When I lived near the ocean, it sat in the sand at the end of the path that led to the beach. Before dawn, I walked by it every morning. I was drawn to its splintered wood and rugged beauty. I wondered who had left it there. Among the seagrass, it seemed strong yet weary and worn.

The wooden chair became a focal point of many of my photos; something beckoned me to focus on the light surrounding the old chair. The emptiness represents loss and grief. In my own journey, it portrays a divorce, the passing of my beautiful mother, and the sudden and tragic death of a husband.

But it also depicts any kind of loss—perhaps a loss of innocence, the death of a child, the end of a career, a decrease of physical mobility, or the devastation of a dream.

Look higher and turn your gaze beyond the chair. The sun, rising on the horizon, brightens the picture. The radiant light symbolizes hope—the kind of hope that always is there, just like the dawning of a new day.

Jesus is our hope. In fact, He is our only hope.

Jesus is the one who redeems pain, heals lives, and turns sorrow to joy.

1

Walk With Me

How many times have you heard me cry out "God please take this?"
How many times have you given me strength to just keep breathing?

—PLUMB, "NEED YOU NOW"

My mother named me well. Meredith is Welsh and means "guardian of the sea."

Before dawn, I stand on the sand where the water meets the shore and look out over the vast expanse, taking it all in. I adore the ocean breeze on my skin and the sound of the seagulls. The dancing waves are enchanting, and the sun cresting over the horizon never fails to bring a smile to my face.

Truthfully, the ocean ministers to me.

The Virginia horse country claims my roots, but the northeastern coast of Florida is my home. I have a deep love of horses in my bones, and I often run to the ocean to meet the sunrise. Maybe that's why I'm most content astride a horse or on the beach—or even better, galloping the length of the shoreline. The steady pounding of a horse's hooves and the rhythm of the waves are melodies to my ears.

God meets me at the beach. My soul feels absolutely at home walking the shore at sunrise. As the day breaks, hope wells up inside me. I enjoy watching the master artist paint the sky, and I soak in the warmth of the rising light.

My heart carries some hurtful memories; there have been seasons of storm-tossed seas in my life. But the salt air is a healing balm. I dig my heels into the sand, and step after step the world and its problems fade away. Over the pounding of the surf, I hear His whisper. I feel the Lord's presence and know He's walking beside me, even when joy and sorrow meet. Every smile and every tear are noticed by my loving Father.

> *My* heart carries some hurtful memories

The seagulls' morning singing brings a song to my lips. I'm thankful God gifted me with a voice to sing His praises, and that He breathed me into being within the love of a musical family. Melodies and lyrics fill me—songs and psalms, stories and prayers. I mostly listen to praise and worship music now, but my mind often drifts back to the beauty of the old hymns. Music moves me; it is my favorite form of worship, responding with humble thanksgiving to the faithfulness of my Savior, who has never forgotten nor forsaken me.

Along with a passion for music, I enjoy reading and writing. Words leap off pages, probably inherited from my mother, who was a high school English teacher. The songs she wrote for our family to perform are tucked inside my heart in a very special place. Three are included at the end of this chapter.

The book you hold in your hands is my song—a pouring out and back, of sorts, to the waves of grace that sustain me. It is a love story. It traces the route of my life's journey thus far. Like the sprinkling of wrinkles that prove I'm inching toward my fiftieth birthday, these pages reveal years that have been as unpredictable as the ocean, some calm and some stormy.

I'm a mother and a grandmother, yet my heart is as tender as when I was a child. I've weathered a few knee-buckling breakers, as well as some that have knocked me flat and left me gasping for air. First and foremost, I am God's daughter and a woman grateful for the saving grace of Jesus Christ. Every favor and every trial are His.

The sweet innocence of my childhood echoes the words I remember so well: "Jesus loves me this I know, for the Bible tells me so. Little ones to Him belong, they are weak but He is strong." Although I gleaned my faith from my parents, it began to grow as they taught me Scripture from the King James Bible and modeled God's nurturing love.

My memories of church are pleasant. I accepted Jesus as my Savior when I was seven, during an altar call, but it was more a physical action than a response from my heart. I learned more about living a life of faith as I attended Sunday school and youth group, as well as watching my parents live out their faith on a daily basis.

Religion became an intimate relationship for me at the age of twenty-four. The moment my faith became personal remains imprinted on my heart. It was a cool September evening on a church trip that I welcomed Christ's indwelling through the Holy Spirit. I felt an assurance, a blessing, like never before.

It is as true today as it was then: the Lord is my guide, my strength, my peace. Ever since that September night, I have pledged to myself and others, "God has a plan." The role He's writing for me, for my life, is part of His greater love story for the world. It's perfect and purposeful, even through betrayal, divorce, illness, addiction, and death. There are many things I'll never completely understand on this side of heaven. But I look forward to reuniting with my mother and other loved ones one day, and I'll see this truth face-to-face, when all things will be made known. I may not always understand or like God's plan, but I trust the Planner.

> *t*he Lord is my guide, my strength, my peace

Plumb starts her song affirming, "Well, everybody's got a story to tell, and everybody's got a wound to be healed." Like her, I believe there's beauty and meaning in pain. I know that in the hands of God, nothing is wasted.

The words on these pages are simply an act of obedience to the one who inspired me to write them down. The paragraphs are soaked with vulnerability, and this experience has been cathartic and liberating. I pray you will receive the genuine wonder and wonderfulness of God's redeeming love with open hands.

> We are hard pressed on every side, yet not crushed; we are perplexed, but not in despair, persecuted, but not forsaken; struck down, but not destroyed. (2 Corinthians 4:8–9)

Sweet Friend,

   The Master Artist is writing your story too, painting a beautiful horizon of hope just for you—a sign of His redeeming grace. Be encouraged. Remember that God can use it all, and you will survive.

   As my father used to tell me, "Baby, hindsight is twenty-twenty." Maybe, you've heard it as well. As a child, I didn't know what it meant, but if Daddy said it, it must be true. It's easier now to mentally revisit certain life circumstances and think, "Oh, maybe that's why I went through that," or say, "I'm glad God allowed that door to close!"

   My prayer is that within these pages, you will find hope amid His plan and a loving purpose in the middle of your pain.

   I hope you enjoy the words of three of my sweet momma's songs. From your mind to your heart, may the love of God our Father wash over you.

Walk with me ...
Mer

——— "Changed Like a Butterfly" ———

Jimi Buck

One autumn day, I watched a caterpillar climb a tree.
He wrapped himself in silk and thread; safe from the world was he.
Then winter came with cold and rain, but he was safe inside.
Then with the spring, a miracle: God made a butterfly.

Amazing grace, how can it be? Oh, praise His holy name.
He's wrapped me in His threads of love; I'll never be the same.
One blessed day, I'll see His face. He'll split the eastern sky.
Then with His shout, I'll fly away, changed like a butterfly.

My life was ruined; I had no hope; a hell-bound road I trod.
But then I met the savior, the blessed Son of God.
He changed my life; I've been set free from this old world of sin.
In Him a new creation, I have been born again!

Amazing grace, how can it be? Oh, praise His holy name.
He's wrapped me in His threads of love; I'll never be the same.
One blessed day, I'll see His face. He'll split the eastern sky.
Then with His shout, I'll fly away, changed like a butterfly.

The Bible tells of mystery and how we'll all be changed.
Mortal to immortal, it cannot be explained.
But I will be like Jesus and reign with Him on high.
How can I doubt His promises? I've seen a butterfly.

"The Pearl of Great Price"

Jimi Buck

At the bottom of the ocean, a tiny oyster
lay wounded by a grain of sand.
It seemed it was all over, as its life just slipped away.
Then, a miracle began ...

Layer upon layer of its essence wrapped around
that tiny stone embedded in its side,
Transforming something hurtful into something rare:
A pearl, the pearl of great price.

Down from heaven's glory, the Savior came
to be, wounded by mortal man.
It seemed it was all over as they nailed Him to a tree.
Then a miracle began ...

Layer upon layer of His blood was wrapped around the very ones
who pierced Him in the side,
Transforming something sinful into something rare:
A pearl, the pearl of great price.

The pearl, the pearl of great price, purchased by our Lord Jesus Christ,
Wrapped up in His blood, transformed by His love.
The pearl, the pearl of great price.
One day in heaven's portal, a bride in spotless
white will stand before a gate of pearl.
There she will be united with the one who bled and died,
Ransomed for this sinful world.

Layer upon layer of His love will wrap around
whosoever on His name has cried,
Transforming something mortal into something rare:
A pearl, the pearl of great price.

—— "The Alabaster Box" ——

Jimi Buck

A woman came to Jesus and knelt before Him there.
Her tears fell on His dusty feet; she wiped them with her hair.
Her repentant heart was aching for things that she had done.
She broke a box of ointment and anointed God's dear Son.

So, break the alabaster box and spill love's precious ointment.
Mingle it with tears to cleanse your troubled soul.
Just break the alabaster box and say, "My Lord, I love You."
He will give you joy, mend your heart, and make you whole.

In love and deep compassion, the Savior saw her sin.
He knew the life that she had led, her sorrow deep within.
But He said, "Because you love Me and prove it willingly,
Your sins, they're all forgiven; your faith has set you free."

The Savior's heart was broken, as He died for you and me.
His blood, like healing ointment, flowed down from Calvary.
And I know that God the Father shed great tears of sorrow when
His only Son beloved paid the price for all our sins.

So break the alabaster box and spill love's precious ointment.
Mingle it with tears to cleanse your troubled soul.
Just break the alabaster box and say, "My Lord, I love You."
He will give you joy, mend your heart, and make you whole.

2

Safe Harbor

I've anchored my soul in the Harbor of Hope,
where the peaceful waters of His love flow.
A place of rest and refuge from the howling winds that blow,
A haven from the hurricanes that rage against my soul.
Jesus is my Harbor of Hope.

—THE RUPPES, "HARBOR OF HOPE"

My story begins on August 4, 1969. It was one of the hottest days of the year in Manassas, Virginia. I am a middle child, and I like to think I was a pleasant surprise.

I was the fourth of six daughters born to Sidney and Jimi Buck. The first two, Phoebe and Ellen, were born sixteen months apart; Amanda came along four years later. I arrived two years after Amanda. I can imagine my parents' disappointment when I looked up at them with long lashes and the all-too-familiar girl parts. Momma and Daddy just knew in their hearts God would have blessed them with a boy; that was the plan, anyway. But as the old saying goes, "If you want to hear God laugh, tell Him your plans."

Six years later, Kimberly was born. The youngest, Patricia, joined our family four years later, on my tenth birthday. She's never lived down the total wreckage of my special day. For years we heard the tale of when Daddy found out she was yet another beautiful baby girl. When he walked into the delivery room and heard the news, he shook his head and, with tears in his eyes, turned and walked out. He wasn't insensitive, just disappointed.

Our father loved all six of his girls well. In fact, he taught us to ride horses, shoot guns, and kick butt if we ever had to. Momma prayed *a lot*. Most of my sisters loved the outdoors and getting dirty. I was a cross between tomboy and girly-girly with long blonde hair. I ran everywhere I went, and my feet always were bare and dusty.

I lived the first six years of my life on a thoroughbred farm, where our dad trained racehorses and our mom broke them for riding. She hardly weighed more than a hundred pounds, and she never thought twice about jumping on the back of one thousand pounds of horseflesh. Mom fondly referred to riding these amazing animals as "like riding a locomotive." She also would breeze them (exercise them on the racetrack) once they were ready.

Of course, I began riding my own horse at a very young age. It was my very first happy place. In fact, one day my Mema lost me. She searched the house and yard, and when she finally found me, I was on my pony, Tiny Tim. I was facing backward with my head on his rump, sound asleep.

Sometime after second grade, we moved to a little town in northeast Florida that was about thirty miles inland. Mom eventually became a high school English teacher, and Dad was a foreman at a dairy farm. Later, he became a deputy with the sheriff's office; he retired as a captain after serving the county for twenty years.

We lived in a small, three-bedroom, two-bathroom home. Six girls shared two bedrooms and one bathroom. We slept in bunk beds, sharing beds until the two oldest left home. Our bathroom was busy. No, it was grossly overcrowded *every* morning. Nevertheless, we were a tight-knit family and loved each other immensely (unless one of us used all the hot water). The Buck household rarely was quiet. We laughed a lot, fought some, and played outside every day.

Some years, we had a television. Birthdays were not expensive parties with friends but family dinners featuring the birthday girl's favorite meal (within reason) and a homemade cake. I never expected, or received, extravagant gifts for my birthday or at Christmas; it was disappointing at times to just get an orange, a candy cane, and a pair of socks in my stocking. But I always knew Momma and Daddy did the best they could. In high school, I had to do small jobs in the neighborhood to earn money in order to attend events.

My childhood was not filled with prestige and wealth, but it overflowed with love. Like the wood pilings under the docks at the marina, the foundation of my childhood was strong and sturdy.

> *L*ike the wood pilings under the docks at the marina, the foundation of my childhood was strong

Sidney and Jimi were well-known about town and very involved in the small Baptist church we attended. Daddy and Momma lived the same faith at home as in public. They led us in prayer before every meal, and we often had family Bible study at night. Many evenings we sang around the piano. We were a family who loved the Lord, and He was a very real presence in my life as far back as I can remember.

Mornings before sunup, I'd crawl out of my bed to go to the bathroom, and my dad would be sitting at the kitchen table reading his Bible. Mom was ready to answer any why questions I had, such as, "Why do I have to be nice to her, when she's always mean to me?" and she backed up everything she told me with Scripture. "Love your enemies, do good to those who hate you" (Luke 6:27). "If your enemy is hungry, feed him; if he is thirsty, give him a drink" (Romans 12:20).

Momma also was a singer and songwriter. The Singing Buck Family performed at churches all over the southeast. We originally sang southern gospel songs written by others; our first record was a compilation of those. Once my mom had written more than thirty songs of her own, we performed only her music and produced two more albums. All eight of us either sang or played an instrument. When I was young, I sang a solo once in a while and played my beloved maracas. As a teen and into adulthood, I sang alto and broke out the tambourine on the upbeat tunes.

On these occasions, I dressed girly. My older sisters wore matching dresses, and I was so excited when I was finally old enough to wear an identical dress instead of a little girl's dress. My favorite was a long dress with flowing sleeves and a belt with a butterfly buckle. I felt a lot like a butterfly when I wore it.

It also was special because Momma loved butterflies. The very first song she wrote was "Changed like a Butterfly." She told us she was sitting in Sunday school one morning, and "God just poured the words" into her heart, flowing so fast. She quickly jotted down the words on a napkin she pulled from her purse. Each of her songs was a beautiful picture of God's love for His children.

I loved listening to my parents share their testimony of God's mercy and grace during our performances. When Mom sang, I was mesmerized. She praised God with a passion I'd never seen before. Momma loved to worship the Savior. She lifted her voice to her Father in heaven with a smile, and often tears streamed down her face. She taught me to worship without ever knowing it, because she sang to an audience of One.

The Bucks slowly stopped performing as each of us girls grew up, got married, and followed different paths. Singing with my family is a time in my life I always will cherish. The hymns and songs are carved deep into my soul. At night, I still often fall asleep humming and wiggling my toes under the sheet to the sweet melody.

Wondering whether my parents were happy never entered my mind; I knew they were. They adored each other and always had each other's backs. They had endured some personal battles before they started having children, and their love had a strong foundation and very deep roots. Even though I saw them face trials together, they never

> *W*ondering whether my parents were happy never entered my mind; I knew they were.

yelled at each other (not in our presence, anyway). They hunkered down and prayed together through every challenge that arose.

Our parents were the picture of true love and determination. They taught their six girls to love God, be honorable, work hard, and fight for the things we knew to be right. Daddy and Momma were married for more than fifty years, until my mom died at the age of sixty-nine from breast cancer in 2010. Daddy had to lean into Jesus for comfort and hope after she died. Momma was finally in the arms of the Savior.

> Whoever dwells in the shelter of the Most High will rest
> in the shadow of the Almighty. I will say of the Lord, "He
> is my refuge and my fortress, my God, in whom I trust."
> (Psalm 91:1–2 NIV)

Sweet Friend,

Childhood memories can be priceless or painful. Perhaps you didn't grow up in a loving family like I did, and for that I am so sorry. Can you remember a person who nurtured and encouraged you, such as a teacher, a coach, or a neighbor? Someone who made you feel worthy and brought a smile to your face? If he or she is still alive, reach out and say thanks. God knew you needed that person; he or she was His gift to you.

But remember that people inherently disappoint. God created you with soul space designed only for Him to fill. He is waiting to be whatever you need Him to be for you, and it's never too late to ask. He wants to hear the prayers (even if they are merely groans or whispers) from your heart.

Find a safe harbor in Him.

Mer

Have you ever thought your life or current situation is too messed up for you to show your face in church? Do you think you need to get some things in your life right before you begin to pray?

God wants you just as you are. In the Bible, Jesus says, "Come to me, all you who are weary and burdened, and I will give you rest" (Matthew 11:28). He doesn't say *if* or *when* you have it all together. The churches I know are filled with nothing but broken, imperfect people—including those who are called to ministry. Everyone messes up; everyone is a sinner who will never reach complete holiness.

People who go to church, know a few Bible verses, and pray certainly haven't "arrived." Those who think they have arrived are mistaken.

Trust me, you can run straight into Jesus's arms, especially when you feel too angry, too sad, or too unworthy of His love. That's when He does His very best work. God entered this world in a dirty stable and slept in a feeding trough. The Light of the world came in the darkness for those who recognize they need a Savior.

Dressed not in royal robes but in simple cotton, Jesus said to a crowd, "It is not the healthy who need a doctor, but the sick. I have not come to call the righteous, but sinners" (Mark 2:17 NIV).

Everyone falls short of being holy; sin is part of living on this earth. There's the obvious stuff (abuse and murder) and also the not-so-obvious sins (bigotry, envy, gossip, pride).

God sees it all and wants it all. He wants you to trust Him with it. Here is the beautiful thing: the closer you get to Christ, the more like Him you become. If you think you're in bad of shape, the timing is perfect. Come to Jesus just as you are. Don't stress about not having your life cleaned up. He wants to heal you and mend your broken heart. He will pursue you, but He won't force you.

The door is always open. Seeking God is about a relationship—an intimate friendship that is full of forgiveness and grace, mercy, and peace.

——— Deep Breath ———

Throughout my school years, I would run to my mom if I was worried about something, or if I had a big homework project due. Sometimes she would ask, "Darling, how do you eat an elephant?" Then she'd always answer her own question: "One bite at a time."

Her nugget of wisdom is something I often recall when I face monumental tasks. I have to step back from my overachieving multitasking, take a deep breath, and focus on doing one thing at a time.

God instructs us similarly. "Be still, and know that I am God; I will be exalted among the nations, I will be exalted in the earth!" (Psalm 46:10) Are you like me? Do you sometimes get so busy trying to fix something or make everything fall into place that you completely leave God out of it or miss what He is trying to teach you? Especially when what's in front of you is daunting, a huge challenge, or an issue where you feel so very small? If you are like me, then you tend to panic and become fearful.

Here's the deal: I just want the elephant gone now—outta here! If I don't take the time to seek God in the situation, then I'm trying to do His job. I'm relying solely on myself. Do I not trust the Almighty? Is He not more capable and powerful than me? Read about timid Gideon in Judges 6 and then find out how God uses him to defeat the Midianite army in Judges 7. Consider David the shepherd boy against Goliath the giant (1 Samuel 17). And there's also Daniel in the lions' den (Daniel 6).

You will always have elephants in your life. Maybe it's a seemingly overwhelming project at work, a relationship that's creating anxiety in your life, a debt, an illness, or a wayward child. God knows every detail of your situation, and He wants you to lean into Him. God is faithful and trustworthy. Nothing is impossible in His kingdom.

Right now, stop, take a deep breath, square your shoulders, look the elephant in the eyes, and be still. God's got it.

—— Default Focus ——

My earliest childhood memories include riding a horse. The world around me fades away, and I become one with the horse. All the heartache and problems of the world are momentarily forgotten as I completely focus on the one thousand pounds of horseflesh beneath me.

Often I think of my daddy as I break into a nice, steady canter. I remember the many times he'd tell me, "Baby, when you're on or around your horse, always pay attention and stay focused. If you don't, you or someone else might get hurt." It's still wise advice. I strive to focus only on the present moment, and when I do, all seems right with the world. What do you focus on when you are alone with your thoughts? It's common to rehearse life's disappointments and problems. That's where Satan wants you to stay, going over the "If only ..." and "What if ...?" scenarios of the past and the unknowns of future.

But with God as your default focus in the present, you can breathe easier. He is the air that fills your lungs, your breath of life. The story of Job in the Bible is about the temptation to believe Satan's lies. Afflicted and under assault, Job claims in faith, "The Spirit of God has made me, and the breath of the Almighty gives me life" (Job 33:4). Turn your focus to gratitude. Train your mind to count blessings instead of disappointments. The Bible says you have access to divine power that can "take captive every thought" (2 Corinthians 10:5 NIV) in order to demolish anxiety and fear.

Reading Scripture is one way to develop contentment. Learn to focus on how much Jesus loves you and all He wants to offer you. Peace in the present is found there. "But blessed is the one who trusts in the Lord, whose confidence is in Him.... like a tree planted by the water that sends out its roots by the stream. It does not fear when heat comes; its leaves are always green. It has no worries" (Jeremiah 17:7–8 NIV). When difficult times are at hand, you won't be uprooted. I have experienced a lot of distress throughout my life. Only with Christ as my guide, my default focus, have I been able to be okay. He has a plan for you too. Believe it. When you are distracted by pain, turn your attention to Jesus. Stand firm in His love and let Him heal your heart.

3
Sandcastles

I have won and I have lost,
I got it right sometimes
But sometimes I did not.
Life's been a journey;
I've seen joy, I've seen regret.
Oh and You have been my God
Through all of it.

—COLTON DIXON, "THROUGH ALL OF IT"

Little girls often dream of fairytale marriages. Princesses are swept off their feet by handsome princes and ride off to kingdoms of happiness and prosperity. Their homes are fortresses with long, winding staircases that lead heavenward. Love is professed over and over again on moonlit balconies, and romantic nights produce perfect children who play on grassy lawns.

As I walk the beach, I reflect on my childhood fantasies of having a marriage just like my parents. (Well, minus a few children. No way was I going to try to raise six—too much work and noise!) I remember the white Cinderella-style fluffy wedding dress I wore thirty years ago. It makes me smile; I certainly felt like a princess.

I fell madly in love when I was sixteen. Flirtatious and funny boys caught my eye in high school, but I only agreed to date a couple of them. Robert, however, was musically gifted and intriguingly sarcastic— familiar territory for me with five sisters. We started dating when I was a senior. He was two years older than me and already out working. At the age of nineteen, on April 15, 1989, I said, "I do," with the full intention of being married for life. I wanted more than anything to be a wife, and to love and be loved.

> *I* wanted more than anything to be a wife, and to love and be loved.

I tried to love and nurture my new husband in a way that I felt he had missed. Sadly, his mother had died when he was twelve, and his father never remarried. Robert Sr., a wonderful person and high-ranking military man, did his best to love his son. I came into the marriage desiring to feel seen and valued, which was attention I always had craved from my dad. I thought we would complete each other, and in my naiveté, I believed I could teach him to love in the way my heart so desperately longed for.

Robert was a police officer, and I worked in banking. We lived in the same town as where we'd graduated high school and had a small, rented townhouse in Fernandina Beach. Finding a church that suited our style was easy, and we found a home and a shared passion in the music ministry. He played the drums and sang; I was a vocalist.

We attended church weekly, and I often felt the Spirit move. But something still was missing for me. As a child, I had gone through the motions of receiving salvation and living rightly under God. I was doing the work of the Lord, but I had not made Jesus the Lord of my life.

I received a precious gift one night in September 1994. We went with our church to Roanoke, Virginia, to be a part of the annual Blueridge Baptist Church Jubilee Revival. Our pastor delivered the sermon, and during that evening's invitation, he said, "God is speaking to someone here."

I heard the Lord whisper to me, "It's you." At that moment, I wholly received Christ as my personal Savior. God's timing was (and always is) perfect. His omniscient sovereignty and faithfulness washed over me, and I was awed. We sang "Amazing Grace" to close the evening service.

Although it seemed I had sung that song a million times since I was a little girl, it was new to my ears. The words "How precious did that grace appear, the hour I first believed" brought tears of both release and joy. I wept with gratitude and hope.

Our daughter, Jimi, was born early in the marriage in 1991, and Bobby followed eighteen months later. Not yet twenty-five, I was a wife, mom, employee, and part-time student. I was very tired. When Robert worked nights, I'd tuck the kids into bed and hit my pillow too. Often rest eluded me. I would listen to the police scanner on the bedside table and imagine all sorts of bad things. We tag-teamed a lot. There were many times we would meet in the late afternoon and pull over on the side of the road to exchange quick hellos and move the children from his police car to my car.

When Jimi and Bobby were in school, it was homework, cheerleading, volleyball, basketball, and baseball. I tried to be the best wife and mom I could be. Everything I did to win my husband's attention and approval seemed futile, and I was frustrated much of the time. Outsiders saw our marriage as picture-perfect. Disney vacations created happy memories. But in the marriage, I felt unseen, unworthy. I later learned that it was unfair of me to put my self-worth and joy on his (or anyone's) shoulders and expect to be made whole.

The mortgage business, however, was booming in the early 2000s, and I enjoyed financial success and working with satisfied customers. Thankfully, my job provided for our home and lifestyle, and Jimi and Bobby were healthy and carefree. This was a source of happiness for me in my early thirties. Whether in the living room or the bedroom, there was plenty of activity. Yet, I felt alone.

For seventeen years, we tried to fill our own voids. My "happily ever after" ended, as did the marriage. I was just thirty-six. Yesterday's castle was now unrecognizable, much like when a child's sand fortress is washed away with the tide.

There was never going to be a good time to endure divorce, and for Jimi, fifteen, and Bobby, thirteen, it was brutal. Years of heartache and the betrayal I felt left me empty.

I felt guilty about what we had done to the children, and it nearly tore me apart. I felt like God no longer would use me—a woman with a big "D" stamped on her forehead. I was broken. I was a failure. No one would ever want me.

Walking through that season of bitterness was miserable. I was the living picture of the saying "Unforgiveness is like drinking poison and hoping the other person dies," and I was gulping down the poison.

After many years, the biggest takeaway for me was this: a God-honoring marriage is built on love, respect, and the firm foundation that only a relationship with Jesus offers. In addition, wound-healing and soul-filling love comes only from the Savior. And I had one final choice to make: I either could hold onto the hurt, or I could forgive and move forward.

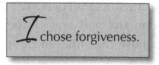

I chose forgiveness. "When everything in you wants to hold a grudge, point a finger and remember the pain, God wants you to lay it all aside," says R. T. Kendall in his book *Total Forgiveness*. It also taught me that the change of heart and resulting peace I wanted wasn't something I could make happen. It only would come from Him.

The waterfall of calm that washed my tears away began to flow when I placed all the pain at the feet of Jesus. I asked the Holy Spirit to empower me to forgive and extend grace over and over again, not only to those who had hurt me but also to myself.

> Therefore whoever hears these sayings of Mine, and does them, I will liken him to a wise man who built his house on the rock: And the rain descended, the floods came, and the winds blew and beat on that house; and it did not fall, for it was founded on the rock. But everyone who hears these sayings of Mine, and does not do them, will be like a foolish man who built his house on the sand: And the rain descended, the floods came, and the winds blew and beat on that house; and it fell. And great was its fall. (Matthew 7:24–27)

Sweet Friend,

Trust and be obedient—not always easy, and certainly letting go of the past is a process. I had to learn the hard way that continually looking back into the past made me stumble. Glancing back is necessary for remembrance and learning, yet forward focus is required for growth. Proverbs 16:9 says, "A man's heart plans his way, but the Lord directs his steps."

It's a cliché, but it's true: The windshield is bigger than the rearview mirror for a reason. Ask God to help you forgive those who have hurt you. Or do you need to forgive yourself? He will help. Surrender to His healing. Leaning into Jesus brings a more intimate relationship and steadies your faith walk.

Go ahead. He is waiting, and He has unimaginable peace waiting for you.

Build your castle in His kingdom.
Mer

⸻ A Matter of Heart ⸻

The Beatles song "All You Need Is Love" is a catchy tune and a universal truth. As children, when my sisters and I would fight, Momma would make us hug and tell one another, "I love you." I'm sure she knew that in that moment, we did not feel very loving, yet she wanted us to remember that even in the midst of the battle, we were still family, and we loved each other no matter what.

Even though we are called to love one another, often we're more so concerned with judging the people around us. God *is* love, so it's no wonder the word appears hundreds of times in the Bible (more than three hundred times in the King James Bible, nearly three hundred-fifty times in the New American Standard Bible, and five hundred-fifty times in the New International Version). It's of utmost important in God's kingdom: "And now these three remain: faith, hope and love. But the greatest of these is love" (1 Corinthians 13:13 NIV). Then there's this passionate proclamation: "Above all, love each other deeply, because love covers over a multitude of sins" (1 Peter 4:8 NIV).

Certainly it's easy for me to love kind, "normal" people, and it's much more difficult to dredge up love for those I think are weird or mean—those who make me uncomfortable. However, I'm commanded to love not just inside my safety zone but also outside my box of comfort. Jesus says, "But I tell you, love your enemies and pray for those who persecute you, that you may be children of your Father in heaven. He causes his sun to rise on the evil and the good, and sends rain on the righteous and the unrighteous" (Matthew 5:44–45 NIV).

In many instances, this is extremely difficult. Abusers and murderers too? Yes. With all the atrocities in the world, it's easy for our human minds to justify hatred, but Almighty God calls us to love, forgive, and even minister to cruel, hurtful people. He doesn't say it's easy, but it's necessary. Justice belongs to Him.

Love must be a choice. As we follow the example of Christ, we will grow to be more like Him—more faithful, more hopeful and more loving. He loves us when we are unlovable, He died for us while we were still sinners, and He has gone to prepare a place for us so that we can live eternally with Him.

Thank John Lennon and Paul McCartney for the catchy tune, turn up the volume, and sing along with the love song of the Savior. In fact, put it on repeat.

──── Nothing Less Than Love ────

Many years ago, I met an older gentleman, and he challenged my mind. Although I don't remember his name, I remember the wisdom he shared with me: "Anything less than a loving thought is toxic."

Radical, huh? But the more I think about it, the more it makes sense. It's even in the Bible.

Sin begins in our thought life. Satan is sly and loves to fill our brains with garbage. Negative thoughts create doubt, hateful thoughts create division, anxious thoughts create disbelief, and self-critical thoughts create isolation. But God's Word is the soap for "stinkin' thinkin'." Scripture teaches the remedy for a toxic mind: in the words of the Apostle Paul, "bringing every thought into captivity to the obedience of Christ" (2 Corinthians 10:5). Paul also says,

> Whatever is true, whatever is noble, whatever is right, whatever is pure, whatever is lovely, whatever is admirable—if anything is excellent or praiseworthy— think about such things. Whatever you have learned or received or heard from me, or seen in me—put it into practice. And the God of peace will be with you. (Philippians 4:8 NIV)

Wouldn't it be nice to think beautiful thoughts and speak lovely words most of the time? I can, and you can too. It takes a mind shift. Move your thoughts from this world to God, from scarcity to abundance, from darkness to light.

Try it and see what happens. Think love, be love, and give love.

4

Sea Glass

This is my temporary home, it's not where I belong.
Windows and rooms that I'm passing through,
This was just a stop on the way to where I'm going.
I'm not afraid because I know,
This was my temporary home.

—CARRIE UNDERWOOD, "TEMPORARY HOME"

I remember a beautiful spring day in 2006, when my mom called me twice in a row on a workday (which was unlike her). I stepped out of a meeting to call her back.

"Sweetheart, Daddy and I just left the doctor's office. I have stage four breast cancer."

She continued to talk, but I desperately tried to process those six words. When I zoned back in to the conversation, she was saying something about needing a lumpectomy right away and beginning chemotherapy and radiation. Then, in true Jimi Buck fashion, I heard her say with a smile in her voice, "Don't worry,

> "*Don't* worry, darling. God will work out all the details.

darling. God will work out all the details. I'm not worried, and so you shouldn't be."

The thing is, she meant it. My mom trusted that the same God who had been her lifelong provider and protector would also be her healer.

For four years, I watched my mom walk the arduous road of late-stage cancer and the "treatment" that was the protocol to extend her life. Through it all, my sweet, optimistic mother never lost her humor, and not once did her faith or trust in the Savior waver. The cancer journey was very difficult for my introverted dad, and my mom wanted to make it easier on him. My older sister, Phoebe, shaved mom's head when her hair began to fall out. Mom told my dad that this was his chance. "Daddy, pick any color you want," she said in her witty way.

Standing in the wig store, my dad said to Momma, "I think I want a blonde, a brunette, and a redhead." Like they always had, they made the best of a hard situation.

One afternoon, I went to see my parents, and as soon as I walked in the door, my dad said, "Me and Momma have a new song." He already had it cued up to play, and moments later the twangy voice of Randy Travis singing, "I'm Gonna Love You Forever" floated through the air.

I smiled and said, "That's sweet, Daddy."

"No, listen to this verse," he said. My quiet dad wanted my mom to know he loved her no matter what. And as Randy crooned, the strong and tough-as-nails Sidney Buck pointed at the radio and said through his tears, "This part right here."

"They say time take its toll on a body, makes a young girl's brown hair turn gray. Well, honey, I don't care, I ain't in love with your hair and if it all fell out, well, I'd love you anyway."

I had credited my mom with most of my life lessons up to this point. My dad was the disciplinarian, whereas mom always was sharing an antidote or one of her sayings in order to create a teachable moment. However, in this moment, my stoic, earthly father was shining the light of the heavenly Father and making an eternal impact.

> *My* parents leaned into each other and together pressed into Jesus

So began another layer of love between my mom and dad. When I thought they could not comfort, support, and encourage each other more, I watched them do it. My parents leaned into each other and together pressed into Jesus, the author and finisher of their faith. "A cord of three strands is not quickly broken" (Ecclesiastes 4:12 NIV).

Momma was my best friend and a role model like no other. Once again, she didn't disappoint. She battled cancer with the sword of faith. During the last few months of her life, I spent Wednesdays with her. I asked her questions because I wanted to be prepared. Nobody else was asking her what the doctor was saying, in terms of her life expectancy. Daddy knew, but he had a difficult time talking with us about her death. He couldn't fathom life without her.

One day I asked point-blank, "Mom, when do you think you will die?"

With a twinkle in her eye, she answered, "Sweet darling, I may have cancer, but you could be hit by a truck today. When we are going die is known only by God."

Another time I asked, "Mom, are you afraid of dying?"

She smiled as tears streamed down her face. "No, sweetheart, I'm not afraid to die. Heaven is going to be marvelous! I just worry about your daddy. I hate to leave him here, but I am ready to see my Savior."

On May 14, 2010, I sat at the foot of my mother's bed as she breathed her last breath and was received into the arms of the heavenly Father in her eternal home. I had prayed for four years asking God to heal my mom from the cancer in her body, and for four years, I felt like God wasn't answering my prayer.

As I lay at my precious mom's feet, having felt defeated in my prayers for healing, I cried. I wept for the loss of my mother—caregiver, companion, the only one who had ever loved me unconditionally, and my best friend. I questioned God. This woman had loved Jesus more than anyone I had ever known, and He had just allowed her to die.

As I cried, the Holy Spirit whispered to me, "She is healed."

Immediately, pieces of scripture came to mind. Later that day, I opened my Bible and found the comfort I sought. When Mom had talked about death, she quoted, "We are confident, yes, well pleased rather to be absent from the body and to be present with the Lord" (2 Corinthians 5:8). I also remember many times when she talked about heaven, and she reminded people, "And God will wipe away every tear from their eyes; there shall be no more death, nor sorrow, nor crying. There shall be no more pain, for the former things have passed away" (Revelation 21:4).

Today, as I think about my mom's life testimony, I know she is completely healed. In fact, she received her heavenly reward! She didn't want to leave my dad in this old world because she knew how wonderful heaven would be. Mom longed for her eternal home, where there would be no more pain, tears, or sorrow, but only living in the presence of Christ.

God answered my prayers after all. Maybe not how I would have done it, as selfishly I wanted her healed here on earth. He did, however, answer my pleas perfectly. Do I miss my mom? Yes, every day. Yet I smile knowing she is worshipping at the feet of Jesus, completely whole, completely healed.

For me, the grief of missing my mom felt like a sailing vessel with a broken mast. My sails were lifeless; I felt dead in the water. My mom was my go-to, my phone-a-friend lifeline. She always was my compassionate comforter, trustworthy confidant, and wise counsel. To me, the most beautiful human on this earth was gone, and I was never to hear her call me darling again.

> To me, the most beautiful human on this earth was gone, and I was never to hear her call me darling again.

Even years after her death, I would pick up the phone to call her just as I always had on my way to work in the morning. There remain days I wish I could call her and share all that is on my heart. When I am sad or disappointed, I imagine her saying, "My darling, this too shall pass," or, "All will be well."

Just a few months ago, I attended an award meeting. On the way back to my car afterward, someone stopped me and asked, "This may sound crazy, but is Jimi Buck your mother?"

I said, "Yes, she is."

"I knew it! You have her smile," she responded. The woman had been one of my mom's students and had moved out of town. She hadn't known of mom's death. I cried all the way back to work, missing her. Yet, my heart was filled with joy because she was not forgotten.

I carry her smile with me.

> And we know that all things work together for good to those who love God, to those who are the called according to *His* purpose. (Romans 8:28)

Sweet Friend,

Have you ever lost someone who was precious to you? Maybe a parent, spouse, or child? There is no other pain quite so excruciating. It may not feel like it at the time of your grievous loss, but God sees your pain and feels it with you, and He has never left your side. David reminds us, "Yea, though I walk through the valley of the shadow of death, I will fear no evil; for You are with me" (Psalm 23:4). He is holding your hand and sometimes even carrying you through the valley. So, just be held.

I am excited to share with you devotions about some of the things my mother taught me. Those who knew my mom know that she was always on the lookout for a teachable moment. She was a wise woman and was quick to speak truth in love.

Lean into the lessons.
Mer

──── Seen but Not Heard ────

When we were children, Momma sometimes would tell my sisters and me, "Children should be seen and not heard." She didn't want mute children. She simply wanted us to be respectful and less rowdy when she had company or needed some peace and quiet. As a child who craved attention, I didn't like her words; I liked to be heard.

Similarly, as a child of God, there have been times in my walk when I knew He was there. I knew in my heart He could see me. But I questioned whether He could hear me, because God did not answer my requests within my timeframe. (I chuckle as I write this. Here I am, the creation, wanting the Creator to be at my beck and call.) I recall Daddy telling me that God answers us three ways: yes, no, and wait a while. It was during the waiting that I sometimes felt like God wasn't hearing me.

Quite the opposite was true. The loving Father heard me and was allowing me to learn to trust His timing. God was building my character and enlarging my faith. "My brethren, count it all joy when you fall into various trials, knowing that the testing of your faith produces patience" (James 1:2).

When you feel like God has gone radio silent, know that He hasn't. He most assuredly sees you and hears you. Scripture declares, "Your Father knows what you need before you ask Him" (Matthew 6:8 NIV). Isn't that reassuring? As a matter of fact, it should take the pressure off. God's got whatever is troubling you.

Take a deep breath and know God's timing is always perfect. He is never late. Keep trusting, believing, and praying. He's all ears.

—— GREENER GRASS ——

I did not grow up in a wealthy home. My parents were loving yet strict. To say I never got away with anything is an understatement. There were times I wasn't allowed to buy something or go somewhere my classmates were able to go. When I expressed my opinion that I wish we were rich or that they weren't so strict, my mom always told me we were rich in love.

"My darling, the grass may look greener in the neighbor's yard, but if you look closely, it is usually directly over the septic tank," she said.

It didn't sit well with me when I was a teenager, but as I have experienced life more, I see what Momma meant. It's easy to gaze at someone else's life, especially through the lens of social media, and think a situation is better than yours, maybe even perfect. Upon closer inspection, you realize someone's stuff may not be as flawless as you envisioned. Scripture warns, "A sound heart is life to the body, but envy is rottenness to the bones" (Proverbs 14:30).

Looking back, I realize I had so very much for which to be thankful. My less-than-emerald yard wasn't so bad after all. What about you?

Comparison isn't realistic or beneficial. When you obsess over what you don't have (or think you don't have), you forget to thank the heavenly Father for all of the blessings He is providing. Don't let envy grow weeds in your heart.

—— Glass Houses ——

I was fourteen the first time my mother scolded me with the proverbial, "Sweetheart, those who live in glass houses should not throw stones." I had just told her about someone at school who did something I thought was wrong. Instead of the hoped-for response from my mom, proclaiming me the perfect child and telling me what a good person I was for not doing those things, she busted my self-righteous bubble with truth.

Her words hit their intended mark and got me thinking about my own sins (gossip, lying to my sisters, etc.). I realized it's easy to pick apart another person, because looking inward is quite difficult.

> Why do you look at the speck of sawdust in your brother's eye and pay no attention to the plank in your own eye? How can you say to your brother, "Let me take the speck out of your eye," when all the time there is a plank in your own eye? You hypocrite, first take the plank out of your own eye, and then you will see clearly to remove the speck from your brother's eye. (Matthew 7:3–5 NIV)

Jesus also taught this when a crowd was accusing a woman who had been caught in the act of adultery. The religious leaders told Jesus the law demanded she be stoned for her sin. Instead of condemning her to death, while the crowd awaited His thoughts, Jesus bent down to write in the sand. Then, He said, "He who is without sin among you, let him throw a stone at her first" (John 8:7). He bent down again to write in the sand, and this time when He looked up, every persecutor had dropped his stones and left.

> Jesus straightened up and asked her, "Woman, where are they? Has no one condemned you?" "No one, sir," she said. "Then neither do I condemn you," Jesus declared. "Go now and leave your life of sin." (John 8:10–11 NIV)

Our God is just, but here Jesus chose to be merciful to this woman. I think about the many things I have done wrong and displeased the Father. He commands me to love others as He mercifully loves me. Let's drop the rocks. Rather than being ready to accuse and condemn, live with hands free to reach out in Christlike love.

5
Jumping Waves

Tell your heart to beat again,
Close your eyes and breathe it in.
Let the shadows fall away,
Step into the light of grace.
Yesterday's a closing door,
You don't live there anymore.
Say goodbye to where you've been,
And tell your heart to beat again.

—DANNY GOKEY, "TELL YOUR HEART TO BEAT AGAIN"

I remember going to the beach with my family as a little girl. My sister Amanda would run into the rushing breakers without fear and begin jumping the waves. But I was timid and small for my age. I was intimidated and afraid I would drown.

Daddy would often hold my hand at first if I asked him, and so we walked deeper into the water together. His strong grip helped calm my nerves. Ankles wet, then knee deep. Soon, I was confident enough to jump and play in the surf with my sister. It was so freeing.

After the divorce, I felt much like that scared little girl. I wanted to jump the waves again, to go out and laugh with friends, to be carefree and have fun. But I needed the guidance and strength of the Father to lead the way.

Even though I was the one ready for the marriage to be over and had been planning to leave for some time, the divorce was difficult. It was a scary time for Jimi, Bobby, and me. I rented a condo near the beach, which was my first taste of coastal living. Little did I know then how much living near the water was just what my soul needed during that season spent deep in the throes of healing.

I wanted to hide and lick my wounds, but a disappearing act isn't easy in a small town. I mustered up a bit of courage every morning and held my head high as I went to work, and as I took Jimi to volleyball and Bobby to basketball and baseball. Sometimes it seemed like the other moms were gossiping and whispering behind their hands, or all eyes were on me because I was the hot topic of conversation. I tried to not let it bother me because I knew the truth. I limped as best I could through those early months of singleness.

During this time, I claimed these words: "If I ascend into heaven, You are there; if I make my bed in hell, behold, You are there. If I take the wings of the morning, and dwell in the uttermost parts of the sea, even there Your hand shall lead me, and Your right hand shall hold me" (Psalm 139:8–10). This Scripture reassured me that no matter the season of my life, God always is and will be with me.

Most people thought I had a lot of friends, but I have just a few intimate girlfriends with whom I share my life. Lots of people in town didn't even know Robert and I had been having problems; I'd tried to protect my family in the hopes that one day, everything would work out.

In His infinite faithfulness, God kept the most amazing friends close to me during my transition. They didn't judge, they listened, and they prayed for all of us. The "couple friends" Robert and I shared were great too, praying for us and not picking sides. They loved us well and respected our privacy.

When the kids were with their dad, I tended to isolate myself, walking the beach to think and pray. I had so many emotions to sort through, fears to talk with Jesus about, and unknowns to face, and so I walked and walked, until the ocean became my dearest friend. The sunrises called to me with God's promises of protection and provision, and each sunset brought the calm of His peace.

The church we had attended together remained important to me. I decided to step away with the hope the kids' dad would continue going. He did for a while, and I was thankful. Our pastor, Jeff, and his wife, Cheri, were good friends, and I knew they always would love and pray for Robert, the children, and me. I began spending Sunday mornings with my parents at the small Baptist church in Callahan that they attended. When Jimi and Bobby were with me, they came too. After church, we went back to my mom and dad's house to eat lunch and hang out. Those Sundays together were a precious time.

Riding the roller coaster of good weeks and not-so-good weeks the first few months eventually slid into a new, steady routine. I did things a little differently as a single mom. I still was fairly strict, and the family values did not change, but I tried to create a less stressful, laid-back environment. For example, Jimi wanted a white Christmas tree the first time it was just the three of us, and so we looked everywhere until we finally found one. I let Jimi and Bobby pick out the ornaments, and they chose bright colors ... and nothing matched. It was wonderfully different!

We ordered Chinese food at least once a week and ate in the living room—a huge hit. After living in the beach condo for six months, we moved to a cute cottage in the center of town. My goal first and foremost was to give Jimi and Bobby love and stability. And I needed it as much as they did.

The one-year anniversary of my divorce came around without fanfare. Although I had thoughts of someday finding someone to spend the rest of my life with, my heart wasn't all that hopeful. I wasn't excited about joining the dating pool. Besides the children, my companions were work, the barn (and riding my horse, Patches), and the TV remote (oh, how I loved having the control!).

But there was one guy in whom I gradually became a bit interested. Lee Lewis and I worked together, and when I realized I had grown attracted to his exuberant demeanor and somewhat zany ways, I was surprised.

I'd met Lee about eighteen months earlier, while I was still married. One afternoon at the office, he walked in with a big smile on his face. He had on nice slacks and a dress shirt with the sleeves rolled up. He was cocky and sure of himself; I was not impressed. *Who is he?* I thought after he walked right up to my desk and extended his hand in greeting.

"Are you the famous Meredith?" he asked.

Not certain how to respond, I replied, "And you are ...?"

Like I should have known, he beamed and said, "Lee Lewis!"

Many women probably would have blushed under the attention of such a good-looking man with olive skin and dark hair, but I was married. That day, I honestly didn't notice his looks, only that he was very sure of himself. It was a busy day, and I didn't have time for his spiel, but I tried not to be rude. I let him stand there next to my desk and heard him out.

Lee also was in the mortgage industry and was opening a new office in town. Although he tried hard to convince me I needed to change offices and work for him, I politely turned him down. The bank I was working for at the time had recently sold, and I already had verbally committed to another bank. I explained this, but that didn't seem to deter Lee.

"Timing is everything," he said. Persistence is one thing he had going for him. Eventually I caved in and joined his team. Lee was kind to everyone in the office and was always quick with a smile and a compliment. He loved to make people feel good about themselves.

Extremely friendly and passionate, Lee made everyone feel like they were his best friend in a very genuine way. He used to quote Teddy Roosevelt: "People don't care how much you know, until they know how much you care."

Lee asked me out on a date a year after my divorce. We had become friends, and I was comfortable around him, so I agreed. We went to a movie with another friend; I enjoyed myself and the easy laughter. Although we worked together, Lee rarely was in the office. When he did come in, generally we were too busy to chat. A short time later, he joined another bank as a commercial lender.

We continued to date, and as time moved forward, I learned more about Lee. Even though he had shared with me early on that he was an alcoholic in recovery, as we became better acquainted, I realized what a daily struggle it was for him. Lee regularly attended Alcoholics Anonymous meetings and was devoted to helping others become and stay sober. He was a fitness enthusiast and was in phenomenal physical shape. Lee told me his addictive personality required he focus on healthy ways of living.

He threw himself into whatever ignited his passion: his faith, his daughters, and his friends. Lee loved Jesus. Because of Christ's saving grace extended to him, Lee wanted everyone he met to experience that same grace, and he was not ashamed to share his story with anyone who would listen. He didn't judge others; often he would say, "But God ..." and it reminded me of the Scripture in Ephesians. "But God, who is rich in mercy, because of His great love with which He loved us, even when we were dead in trespasses, made us alive together with Christ (by grace you have been saved)" (Ephesians 2:4–5).

Lee loved his two little girls fiercely and wanted more than anything to be a good daddy to Sarah Katherine, five, and Caroline, three. He did all he could to protect them and lead them to a life of faith. He told me once, "I may not be able to give them all the things money can buy, but I can show them the way to a relationship with Jesus."

Lee and I came from different denominational backgrounds. Lee's Granny Lewis took him to a Billy Graham crusade, and at the age of twelve, Lee dedicated his life to Christ. While growing up, he often attended a Presbyterian church with his parents, however as a young man he strayed from the path of faith. When Lee began his journey to sobriety, he knew that he would need the help of the heavenly Father and leaned into Him. Thankfully, we found an amazing non-denominational, Bible-teaching church together, and I watched Lee's spiritual walk blossom.

We dated for about seven months and then got married in December 2006. As a fifteen-year-old, Jimi struggled with having to share me. She'd had visions of us being like the Gilmore Girls. Bobby, on the other hand, was thirteen and seemed like he could have cared less.

I moved into Lee's house, and we settled in as a blended family with Jimi, Bobby, Sarah Katherine, and Caroline with us when they weren't with their other parents. Lee's girls lived with their mom about an hour and a half away, and they hung out with us every other weekend. I had my two teens half the time; they rotated a week with their dad and a week with me. Needless to say, some weeks for Lee and me were quiet, and some were filled with beautiful chaos.

"Okay, here is my second chance," I thought, planning to be the best wife, mom, and stepmom I possibly could be. "Everything is going to work out." My heart beamed. Although it wasn't easy, we did our best and made some amazing memories.

Like most marriages, we had our struggles. But we were committed to putting God first, faithfully staying married, and growing old together. Lee and I each had brought some emotional baggage into the marriage. Lee was fighting his own inner demons, and I still was trying to claim self-worth. We worked hard to help each other be the best version of ourselves, and we woke up early in the morning to read the Bible together over coffee. Sometimes we walked the beach at sunrise and would stop to read God's Word and pray.

As he got down on his knees before the sun, the beginning of Lee's prayer was always, "Good morning, God. This is Lee checking in. I am an alcoholic and a dipaholic, so please help me to resist both today. Help me to be the best son, brother, dad, husband, and friend I can be today." Lee told many people he wanted his life to glorify the heavenly Father.

One day before heading out of town, he gave me a five-page letter. In it he wrote, "I wish—no, I pray—God will use me in a way that is justified and pleasing to Him." Lee may as well have written the words of Paul to the believers in Roman: "Therefore, I urge you, brothers and sisters, in view of God's mercy, to offer your bodies as a living sacrifice, holy and pleasing to God—this is your true and proper worship" (Romans 12:1 NIV).

We'd been married for just over seven years when Lee went on a short trip to visit his daughters and attend their softball banquet. Because the real estate market was in full swing that spring on Amelia Island, I stayed behind to work. We talked for a long time as he sat in his hotel room in Lake City that evening. His plan was to come home the next morning.

I awoke to a call from Lee at six o'clock, and he told me he was going to drive to Sarasota instead, to encourage a friend. I was surprised and not pleased. He told me it was his friend's birthday, and he was worried about him and wanted to go cheer him up. We traded texts throughout the day, and at six thirty that evening, he messaged me, "I love you. I miss you." I still wasn't happy he had detoured from our plan, and my response wasn't loving. We both knew the environment of the destination was not healthy for him in maintaining his sobriety.

Lee encouraged me not to worry. He said, "God's got me."

Later that night, I got news that rocked my world and changed the course of my life forever. Lee's friend called to tell me he was dead.

"No! It can't be. He just text me!" I screamed into my phone.

I collapsed to the floor and held my head in my hands, trying not to throw up. When I asked if Lee was in a car accident, I was shocked to hear the details.

"No, Meredith. We were eating dinner, and he choked to death."

When I finally got the whole story, I found out Lee was at his friend's mother's house, celebrating over a birthday dinner. There were twenty-five or so people at the party, and Lee had taken his first bite of beef tenderloin.

Lee loved to eat. Lee loved beef.

His first bite was a large medallion of meat. Apparently when he realized the meat was stuck and he couldn't swallow, he got up from the table and headed to the bathroom. (Caution: If you are choking, *never* leave a crowded room for an isolated one.)

An unsuspecting guest thought he was going to be sick and led him down the hall so he would not be embarrassed. When she realized he was choking, several people tried to do the Heimlich maneuver, but they weren't able to dislodge the meat. Someone called the ambulance, but Lee died in the arms of his friend's mother before the paramedics arrived.

His body was taken to the medical examiner's office because anytime there is an unexpected, in-home death, an autopsy is required. Several days later, the medical examiner called to tell me the piece of meat was lodged so tightly that even if the medics had been on the scene at the time of the incident, they would not have been able to reach or dislodge it. She also said she'd never had had a forty-three-year-old subject with a heart, lungs, and liver as healthy as Lee's. (Much later, this fact would be important for me to remember.)

> So teach us to number our days, that we may gain a heart
> of wisdom. (Psalm 90:12)

Sweet Friend,

Have you ever felt that you had a perfect plan, only to suddenly have it crumble into pieces at your feet? Me too. But, hear me on this: God can take the shattered pieces of our lives and mold those fragments into something precious. Like artists who collect broken shells or glass that wash ashore on the beach and craft the colorful bits into stunning sculptures, He takes what we think is destroyed and useless, and He creates beauty out of brokenness.

I pray everyone who is reading this will find encouragement. I pray they will, by the power of the Holy Spirit, hand over their worries to God, trust His plan and live a life, not paralyzed by fear but energized by faith, sustained by His promises.

Take the hand of your good Father.
Mer

——— Why Worry ———

As I walk the beach some mornings, I marvel at how the skies could change so quickly. Some sunny mornings are bright and beautiful—the weather mild and the ocean calm. And then *bam!*—hours later, the wind is cool and crisp, the misty rain is falling, and the waves are dark and luminous.

What do we really have control over? I wonder. Certainly not the weather. I shout to the wind, "We don't have control over anything!"

Scripture points out this truth: "Can any one of you by worrying add a single hour to your life?" (Matthew 6:27 NIV) There's also the saying "Worry does not empty tomorrow of its sorrow, it empties today of its strength." My personal favorites are, "Don't miss the sun today, worrying about the rain coming tomorrow," and, "Worry doesn't take away tomorrow's troubles. It takes away today's peace."

I can assure you that the job or bank account you depend on, or even the person you think always will be there, is fleeting at best. Nothing is guaranteed or permanent in this life. After my losses, James 4:14 really hit home in my heart: "Whereas you do not know what will happen tomorrow. For what is your life? It is even a vapor that appears for a little time and then vanishes away."

I've seen disappointment, as well as how short life can be. The soul was created by God to be filled only by Him. He is a dependable, trustworthy Father. A relationship with Jesus is fulfilling, and when life gets tough, only His love comforts and sustains.

Now, I pray as the ocean pounds out its praises to the Creator, and I release everything! I give over my children, my granddaughter, my past, my present, and my future to God. I release all the things that Satan uses to try to cripple me with worry. I know every morning, He is the only one giving the grace of new mercies so that I can hold my head high.

But let me be real. I am not so spiritual that I never struggle and am never tempted to worry. At times I do drive home from the beach to get ready for work and begin my day in the world, and my heart starts pounding as thoughts of giving God total control of my life (like it's even mine to give) enter my mind. I have to unclench my grip on the steering wheel and pray, "Okay, Lord. I gave it all to You just a few minutes ago, and now I am having doubts? Please give me the strength to follow through."

His Word whispers back, "My grace is sufficient for you, for My strength is made perfect in weakness" (2 Corinthians 12:9). Often we must give our worries to Jesus ten, a hundred, and even a thousand times a day. Lean into His grace and trust Him.

——— THINGS UNSEEN ———

Life is disappointing. Plans are made, and expectations come into play.

When things don't turn out, spirits sink, and bitterness tries to creep in. There's no way that at sixteen, I'd ever have imagined being divorced at thirty-six after seventeen years of marriage. Or that I'd be remarried for seven years only to end up a widow at forty-three. To say life didn't go as I had planned is an understatement.

Here is the beauty: God was not surprised. In fact, Jesus clearly says, "These things I have spoken to you, that in Me you may have peace. In the world you will have tribulation; but be of good cheer, I have overcome the world" (John 16:33). He doesn't say *if* we encounter trouble. For every valley I walked through, as well as the disappointments and trials I will face in the future, He works for my good to glorify His name.

God is the great Redeemer. Yes, it's easier to focus on the pain rather than any good that comes from it. But consider this: doesn't sorrow often prompt a turning toward God? How often does a particular struggle teach a personal lesson? Don't new, different directions often result in even better outcomes than what was planned? What if a disappointment is protection from something that could have been devastating?

These are what can be seen and experienced. However, redemption often happens through other lives that are changed. A faithful and God-seeking response to a terrible situation often impacts people who are watching from the sidelines—people who see what a relationship with Jesus offers and want that for themselves.

God sees a future we cannot. He can turn disappointment into delight.

I've learned that if I truly believe my purpose on this side of heaven is to glorify God and build His kingdom, then it's not all about me and my little world. I have to consider the bigger picture, the one He sees.

Blame can hurt both sides. I've blamed someone for something and later realized the person didn't do what I had presumed. With misplaced anger and hurt, I've sat and felt horrible after having avoided someone and allowing the relationship to suffer.

Incorrect assumptions also can be unleashed on God. When something unpleasant or tragic happens, God often gets the blame—even if the unpleasant circumstances were a result of poor choices. The outcome? Isolating from family and friends, staying away from church, avoiding prayer, and withholding worship. The mind can conjure up how mean God is for having allowed bad things to happen, thinking that He's distant and doesn't care.

"Why? Why me? Why now?" is the string of questions uttered when darkness threatens, and the reason or answer is rarely clear. Yet God is never surprised by anything that happens. My dad always says, "When you feel like God has abandoned you, turn around. He is standing right where you left Him; He is the same yesterday, today, and forever. God didn't move—you did."

Isn't it easier to trust God when life is going smoothly? As soon as things start going sideways, His sovereignty comes into question. But whereas earthly eyes focus on earthly things, the Creator of the universe has the good of His entire creation in mind. "So we fix our eyes not on what is seen, but on what is unseen, since what is seen is temporary, but what is unseen is eternal" (2 Corinthians 4:18 NIV).

Faith is trusting the unseen. Choose to live a life of expectancy, trusting God has a plan that is good, even if it may not be free from heartache. I have heard it said, "The plan is only as good as the planner," and I know the heavenly Father is the ultimate Planner. He is love, and He is a good, good Father.

6

Riptide

I know someday,
I know somehow,
I'll be okay.
But not right now,
Not right now.

—JASON GRAY, "NOT RIGHT NOW"

Collapsing to the floor in shock. Feeling utterly alone and terrified. Swimming against the current, blinded by tears. I've lived it, and I know what it's like when nothing makes sense.

On the evening of Thursday, May 16, 2013 I was on the couch with a book waiting for a call from Lee because he was out of town. My cell rang at 9:28. His friend said, "Meredith ..." There was a long pause." "Lee is dead."

What? How? Where? Lee was very athletic and the picture of health. He was supposed to live to be an old man, not die at forty-three. My husband was dead. I didn't get to say, "I love you." I never said goodbye. Our last conversation was an argument.

In a matter of seconds, I went from wife to widow. The swirling waves of shock kept crashing over me, and I didn't know which direction to turn. I desperately wanted to grab my mom's hand and have her pull me in close to safety. I needed her to rub my back and assure me everything was going to be okay as I cried an

In a matter of seconds, I went from wife to widow.

ocean of tears. But Momma was dead, and Lee was dead. The dark sea was pulling me under.

Once I could breathe a bit, I called my longtime friend and my pastor's wife, Kara. She and her husband Darryl, jumped in the car and were by my side within twenty minutes. Kara had called Lee's mentor and friend, Billy, and his wife, Lindsay. My living room quickly became a circle of comfort for me and a lifeline of strength.

I knew Lee's girls and their mother, as well as his parents and siblings, had to be told. God provided the courage and strength to make those difficult calls and visits in the middle of the night. Sometime around three o'clock in the morning, I tried to close my eyes. There was no sleep, only the lonely nightmare of despair.

Lee's body was at the morgue four hours away, and so I wasn't able to see it immediately. Several days later, the funeral home in town called to say Lee was "home." No one else in the family wanted to go, but I had to. I needed to see and touch him one more time to really believe he was gone. I prayed for strength as I prepared my heart to see the lifeless body of my husband. I longed for my mother once again.

The heavenly Father heard my prayer, and the phone rang just as I was ready to leave. Of course it wasn't my mom, however, it was one of my dearest friends. In her loving fashion, Judith Boyle had called to see if there was anything she could do to help. When I told her I was headed to the funeral home, she told me to sit tight. She came over in a dash to pick me up.

God knew exactly whom and what I needed. With the love of a mother, she held my hand, prayed with me, and held me when I cried. She even went in to see Lee first to make sure I could handle what I was about to face. Judith eased my fears and assured me Lee looked like he was sleeping peacefully and was smiling.

Sure enough, Lee was smiling, and he looked as if he would wake up any second. Judith encouraged me to take my time, and I did. In my mind, I knew what I saw was simply Lee's shell, but my heart needed to talk, touch, and pray with him one last time. Judith stepped in and walked with me through one of the hardest experiences of my life. I was grateful beyond words.

After making the arrangements for the service, I left the funeral home knowing I had one additional task that needed to get done. I had to find an important document—one I knew was somewhere within an enormous stack of boxes in our storage unit. I had told only my best friend Angie about my dilemma, and she was flying in from Texas the next day with a promise to help look for the proverbial needle in a haystack. The dread of searching for what could have been hours nearly paralyzed me. As I pulled into my garage, I put my head down and pleaded with God for help. "Please don't let it be in box ninety-nine, Lord. I just don't think I have the energy," I prayed. What happened next was otherworldly.

When I got out of my car, I noticed a single white sheet of paper lying on top of Lee's flip-flops, which were by the door leading into the house. When I bent down to pick it up, my mind could barely comprehend what it was or why it was there. It was exactly the document I needed. This may be difficult for some people to believe; it was for me at the time. However, I felt God had heard my prayer and answered in a supernatural way.

The Bible says, "For He will command His angels concerning you to guard you in all your ways" (Psalm 91:11 NIV). Also, "Are not all angels ministering Spirits sent to serve those who will inherit salvation?" (Hebrews 1:14 NIV)

Even though I had been freed from that worry, continuing to prepare for Lee's service was still mind-numbingly difficult. Lee, being the man he was, had once shared with me his wishes. Yet going through pictures for the slideshow (thank goodness his sister Virginia was there to help) and listening to the songs he liked was beyond brutal. It took a few days, but I was determined to get everything just right. Jimi barely left my side, and my sister Amanda was a sentinel at the front door, greeting those who brought food and offered condolences and protecting me from being overwhelmed with callers. My friend Kara coordinated most of the actual service and reception with the help of family and friends, relieving me of that huge task.

Eight days after Lee died, we held his celebration of life. It was a beautiful day, but I didn't want to get out of bed. I wanted to crawl under the covers and never come out, feeling like I had aged twenty years in one week. Only for Lee and his daughters, Sarah Katherine and Caroline, did I put on my big-girl panties and face the day.

The church was standing room only, packed with more than seven hundred people in attendance. Worried about walking into the church with people crying and the huge picture of their dad on the screen up front, the girls held tightly to their mom and me and sat sandwiched between us. Both girls stood bravely during the service, and they each went up front and spoke about how their daddy loved God so much and taught them the importance of having a relationship with Jesus.

My counselor, Dr. Linda Miller, later shared with me how touched and impressed she had been regarding their courage. "Lee equipped his children to be able to walk through grief by pointing them so often to Christ," she said.

Everything about the service was nontraditional. I wore a vibrant royal blue dress instead of black. Our pastor and close friend Darryl preached a salvation message at the request of Lee himself. Our friend Chris sang "The Stand" by Hillsong United. People laughed, cried, and had the opportunity to give their lives to Christ. I thought afterward, *I can only hope my funeral will be as impactful.*

We gathered in the lobby following the service, where normally there would be a reception line. Instead, more people had the opportunity to tell "Lee stories." I felt like I hugged a million necks. I don't think I really saw everyone I spoke with, but friends later told me I'd done well. Obviously I was still in shock and doing what I had to do to get through the day, consoling others in their mourning.

> In the days to follow, I fell into a vortex of grief.

In the days to follow, I fell into a vortex of grief. My daughter and a close family friend, David, stayed with me in the evenings. I couldn't sleep in the bed Lee and I had shared, so I camped out on the couch. Dreams of my second chance and growing old with Lee filled my head. To say my life plan had changed yet again was a gross understatement.

I couldn't get my bearings; some days I felt like I was swimming through pudding, and others felt like I was sinking in quicksand. At times, I didn't think I could take my next breath. The grief often was suffocating.

I questioned God's wisdom and His love for me. I pleaded for answers.

"How could You allow Lee to die, and how do You expect me to endure this?" I asked God to turn back time, to give me just one more chance to tell Lee I loved him, assuring him I wasn't angry. Our last words to each other had been strained.

Wrestling with this, I prayed for sleep so I could forget my reality. But then I'd wake up and remember the nightmare. I went over and over the what-ifs, and sometimes I wished I'd had a warning. I wanted to push rewind, but a blank road ahead was all I could see. Sometimes I barely whispered, "Help me, Father." I knew my faith was the only thing that would get me through. I clung to Christ and did my best to praise Him despite my fear and grief. But in the dead of night, sometimes I would wake up and wonder whether I would survive.

Scripture pointed me to truth. "'For My thoughts are not your thoughts, neither are your ways My ways,' declares the Lord. 'As the heavens are higher than the earth, so are My ways higher than your ways and My thoughts than your thoughts'" (Isaiah 55:8–9 NIV). But, oh, how I wanted God's way to be my way.

My next move was hasty and probably not the smartest, but I needed something to focus on besides my loss. Staying home and being in our space wasn't helpful. I returned to work the week after the service. My co-workers Ben and Bianca were amazing, letting me ease back in and do things that didn't require customer contact. They shielded me from the more stressful situations the mortgage business brings. Ben and Bianca had become like family over the years, and they reacted like the brother and sister they are to me. I will be forever grateful for their love and care; simply getting through the day was a major feat.

In my journal, on day fourteen after Lee's death, I wrote,

> It was a really hard day. I could hardly make it up the stairs after work before I started sobbing, so I just laid down right there. I called out to God for comfort. This Scripture from Psalm 56:8 came to mind. "You keep track of all my sorrows. You have collected all my tears in Your bottle. You have recorded each one in Your book." I told a friend yesterday that I see two choices: (1) curl up in a fetal position and wait to die, or (2) glorify the Savior, knowing His ways are higher than my ways. I know the loving Father cares enough for me to collect

all my tears, so I'm going to choose #2. As Lee Lewis used to say, "It's not easy, but it's the right thing to do."

Others around me got back to their normal routines. It was weird. My world had fallen apart, but the rest of the world was still functioning. The sun kept rising. The woodpecker outside my bedroom window continued drumming his morning tune. People were laughing. I thought many times, *Mer, you are never going to feel joy again. Life as you know it is over.* I was right about one thing: Life as I had planned it was over.

The firsts were the hardest—Father's Day, Lee's birthday, and our anniversary. These days screamed reminders of who was missing. Except for Thanksgiving and Christmas, most people weren't aware of how much I was struggling. Jimi, who had grown very fond of Lee, always remembered the hard days and reached out to me. In fact, there was a role reversal, and she became my pseudomom, hovering like a mother hen and telling me how much I needed her. Jimi insisted on moving in with me as a twenty-three-year-old woman, and we enjoyed an adult mother-daughter friendship. Bobby visited us when he could, and I always wished he could have expressed his sadness more, but like most men he kept it all inside.

On my most difficult days, I went to the beach to face the ocean and cry. The vast expanse of water easily could have been my tears as I attempted to cry myself empty of the grief.

Exactly one month after Lee's death was Father's Day. His daughters and their mom came to church with me. It was a difficult morning, especially for the girls, who saw other dads holding hands with their daughters. Yet I knew in my heart that Lee was looking down from heaven, thrilled that we were worshipping together. Our courage and strength that day came from God. We had chosen not to let the sea of grief pull us under.

> When you pass through the waters, I will be with you; and when you pass through the rivers, they will not sweep over you. (Isaiah 43:2 NIV)

Sweet Friend,

God is for you and will walk with you through your disappointment, heartache, loss, and grief. The verse above from Isaiah is a reminder that there is no escaping trouble in this earthly life. But God is with you every day and in every circumstance. He will even carry you, if necessary.

Have you ever felt like you were running out of strength, or that you couldn't keep your head above the waves any longer? Stop striving, stop struggling. The loving Father is there to catch you and hold you when you feel you can't go on. Surrender to His everlasting arms.

God hears your cries for help. Rest assured in His promise to never turn away from you or leave you—this is His comfort for your weary soul. I pray a few of the things I wrote in my journal that first year after Lee's death may help you during a time of needed encouragement.

Christ reaches to rescue in strong currents.
Mer

—— A Safe Haven ——

July 2013. I headed to Starbucks after leaving the beach this morning. Just before I opened the door, I look down and saw a little bird on the pavement. She was very still and dangerously in the traffic pattern of customers. I bent to take a closer look, careful not to touch her. The little bird was very much alive; her heart was beating fast and hard. She didn't look hurt, just stunned. I thought she must have flown into the Starbucks window. The poor thing didn't know what hit her.

Afraid someone would walk by and accidentally step on her, I put my finger in front of her. The tiny bird stepped on. As I relocated her to a safe patch of grass, I whispered, "I know how you feel, sweet sparrow."

Continuing on my way, I was reminded of a cherished Scripture from my childhood. "Are not five sparrows sold for two copper coins? And not one of them is forgotten before God. But the very hairs of your head are all numbered. Do not fear therefore; you are of more value than many sparrows" (Luke 12:6–7). The little bird had needed a safe place to rest until she could take to the sky once again.

There are days that I too feel stunned and not quite sure what to do next. I long for a quiet place to heal. I am reminded that just as God had allowed me to help one of His little creatures, He lovingly takes care of me.

It's time for sleep. I pray my mind will give in to rest tonight. The Comforter is here—the one who gently whispers in my ear that He is very aware of my tears and my every need.

Jesus is my resting place.

—— Beauty in the Storm ——

August 2013. Lee loved a good storm. Me? Not so much. Lee always opened the windows and the sliding glass door so he could see the ocean and hear the wind and rain. He'd say, "Mer, this calls for a pot of coffee." He celebrated a storm. I would curl up next to him as the lightning flashed and the thunder boomed, and I felt safe.

The past months have been the hardest of my entire life. The pain of missing sometimes physically hurts, so much so that it leaves me crying out to God to wrap His arms around me and hold me during the storm. And the fear. Oh, the fear. It keeps stalking me.

My counselor, Linda, tells me to look at it like fear and I are playing a game of tag. She reminds me of when, as a child, I got all quivery while waiting to be tagged. But once I actually was tagged, the fear left, and I had a feeling of being in control again. I love this analogy and keep thinking about it. I have decided to be still and name my fear of being alone for the rest of my life. I'll let it touch me and feel it, and then it will no longer control me.

"I sought the Lord, and He heard me, and delivered me from all my fears" (Psalm 34:4). I am learning to focus on Jesus rather than my fear.

There is a storm rolling in tonight. I sit with the sliding door open, and I smile. The sound of the rain makes me feel closer to Lee. I keep finding the little notes Lee stashed for me all around the house. Little signs of his presence are popping up for me everywhere. Soon, there won't be any more left.

I'm also discovering daily encouragements from Jesus, the lover of my soul. The Scriptures I have read many times mean so much more to me now, and the peace that fills my heart when I pray is amazing.

Even this storm tonight is a reminder that God paints beauty out of tragedy. I am going to celebrate this life storm and give thanks for His deliverance.

—— Legacy ——

September 2013. *Death* was the word I whispered today as I passed the funeral home. The place was packed with cars, and even though I didn't know who had died, my heart squeezed with sorrow for the people left behind. Life doesn't go on forever. I once heard someone say, "Statistics prove that ten out of ten people will die this year."

Perhaps for some, it isn't as scary, especially if you know where you're going and that it's going to be a holy place without any sickness or tears. My mom wasn't afraid of dying, but she wasn't looking forward to leaving Daddy all alone. Lee and I talked about dying too. He used to say, "I'm not afraid to die. I am just afraid of the process." He was most concerned with being a sickly burden to his loved ones.

For Lee's sake, that never happened. But I was not prepared. I was left without a plan. I'm a major planner (always prepared and even overprepared), and so life has been pulled out from under me. There's no reaching into my magic Mary Poppins bag to get needle and thread to patch my broken heart, or a salve to soothe the burn of my anger over life's unfairness.

There's one thing I've learned I can be prepared for: to meet Jesus face-to-face. Lee had been ready. He had accepted Christ as Lord of his life and was all set to meet the Savior. When his daughters talked about him at the service, they didn't recall his accomplishments in business or all the cool stuff he'd bought for them over the years. Rather, they recounted how much their daddy loved everyone and told everyone about Jesus. They told the entire church about how his favorite saying was, "Girls, God's got it."

There is comfort in knowing where Lee is spending eternity. He was not perfect, but he left a legacy. Oh, that Nichole Nordeman song to Jesus: "I want to leave a legacy, how will they remember me? Did I choose to love? Did I point to You enough to make a mark on things? I want to leave an offering, a child of mercy and grace who blessed Your name unapologetically."

I don't think it's morbid for people to ponder what others will find when they sift through the ashes of a life, or even to consider what kind of eulogy will be spoken, and whether others will be comforted, knowing greetings of "well done good and faithful servant" (Matthew 25:23) were given in heaven.

God, help me be mindful of living and leaving a legacy of faith.

7

Driftwood

Spirit lead me where my trust is without borders,
Let me walk upon the waters
Wherever You would call me.
Take me deeper than my feet could ever wander
And my faith will be made stronger
In the presence of my Savior.

—HILLSONG UNITED, "OCEANS (WHERE FEET MAY FAIL)"

Spring is a particularly beautiful season on the Florida coast. There are days when I think there couldn't be a more perfect place to live.

For me, the month of May is bittersweet. May 8 is Momma's birthday, and sometimes it's also Mother's Day (six times since I was born, and twice since my mom died). May 14 is now Mom's heaven-versary. May 16 is the day Lee died, and May 1 is the day I got married again.

In 2013, just eight days before Lee died, he and I talked about my mom in Heaven. It went something like this.

"Happy birthday, Jimi Buck!" he shouted to the sky.

"Hey, do you think they have birthday celebrations in heaven?" I wondered aloud.

"Hmm, I don't know, sweetheart."

"Nah, I bet they have rebirth day celebrations," I said.

"Heaven is going to be so cool; I can't wait to go there. Hey, if anything ever happens to me, I want my funeral to be awesome," he said emphatically. "Ask Pastor D to preach salvation, because all my fraternity brothers will be there. He can do it in a way that it won't be like cramming it down their throats, but they will get it! Oh, and sing that song I love, 'I'll Stand,' okay?"

"Lee, you're as healthy as a horse! You're going to live a long time. But whatever you say," I agreed.

Remembering that conversation reminds me of the tree branches and limbs that have been washed ashore by tides or waves. This ocean debris often is transformed into appealing works of art. Dry, hardened driftwood provides perches and shelter for birds, and it can become the foundation for erosion-preventing sand dunes. Though once soggy pieces of wood floating aimlessly in the sea, driftwood is remarkable after the storm.

Similarly, as I began to dry out from my painful days and nights of crying, I reflected on all the eternally changed lives because of Jimi Buck and Lee Lewis. Their lives and deaths were not in vain.

I read once, "To have suffered much is like knowing many languages: It gives the sufferer access to many more people." I don't know who said it, but I certainly believe it's true. The loss of my loved ones put me through a level of suffering I never had experienced before. Affliction softens the heart, and mine had been torn and left incredibly tender. Yet in His perfect plan, the Master Potter gently restores the broken pieces.

My woundedness allowed empathy for others' challenges to grow deeper. I became less judgmental and more tolerant, maybe even curious. People's stories are the truth of who they are; appearances often mask the pain inside. God uses pain to bring people together. Scripture says,

> Blessed be the God and Father of our Lord Jesus Christ, the Father of mercies and God of all comfort, who comforts us in all our tribulation, that we may be able to comfort those who are in any trouble, with the comfort with which we ourselves are comforted by God. For as the sufferings of Christ abound in us, so our consolation also abounds through Christ. (2 Corinthians 1:3–5)

Although it might seem easier to suffer in silence, God anoints His people to be bravely vulnerable, walking alongside one another in compassion. Personally, I've found a kinship in shared pain, an unspoken understanding. Those who walk through deep water generally find God reveals His hope through them to others.

As Christians, we know evil abounds in this fallen world. But God is a purposeful and loving father who is involved in every detail of what happens on this earth. When bad things happen, His people are not forgotten and abandoned to fend for themselves. While grieving, I grew to know and love the heavenly Father in a more intimate way. He became my constant companion as I talked to Him about my sadness while walking the beach. I felt His Spirit of healing every time a beautiful sunrise lifted my heart.

> While grieving, I grew to know and love the heavenly Father in a more intimate way.

God also revealed Himself as the Sustainer, helping me stay afloat when the weight of the loneliness almost was too strong. And He also became the Protector, guiding me to safe people and places where I could be myself—not just a widow. The first time I was able to go out with a friend and laugh felt strange but also freeing.

Building a new routine was not easy. After years of being a wife and mother, little by little I began to rediscover Meredith the woman, including what I liked and disliked. I realized I was fairly boring (compared to most single women), and I was okay with that. Waking before the sun came up gave me time in God's Word with a comforting cup of coffee or hot tea. Then I'd go to the gym, catch a breath of the sunrise, and head to work. Later in the afternoon, I'd sometimes stop at Publix (buying food for one was a whole new experience). Evenings were too quiet, so it was not unusual for me to be in bed by eight thirty.

Weekends were filled with reflection and self-care. I spent a lot of time reading (more than one hundred books in the first year). I also wandered around some of the downtown shops and got a pedicure once in a while. I spent lots of time at the barn. Even though I had sold my horse years earlier, sweeping the floor and cleaning the stalls was therapeutic, and sometimes I rode a friend's horse. I eventually bought a new horse, and MoJo became the man in my life. He was spirited and loving—the perfect horse for me, except he never laughed at my jokes. I was mostly content, but a bit lonely for a friend who could share in this new normal with me. The majority of the amazing friends I had were married with families, and I didn't want to impose.

Then it happened. God showed up through a woman I'd met a year or so earlier in the grocery store. She was vaguely familiar, and I sort of remembered her from church.

"Meredith, I am so sorry to hear about your loss, and I'm sorry that I'm just reaching out to you," she said, walking right up to me one morning as I was leaving the gym. The woman explained she had been recovering after having a cancerous tumor removed and was just getting back into her exercise routine. "My name is Lynn, and I have been praying for you. In fact, can I pray with you right now?" And she did, right there in the middle of the gym.

We exchanged phone numbers and talked about getting together for coffee. A few weeks later, we enjoyed getting acquainted and had a long, lovely conversation about our lives, the ups and the downs of raising children, and being middle age. Lynn and I laughed some and cried some, and just like that, a beautiful friendship bloomed.

Lynn was in a season of singleness too, and we became inseparable, nearly glued at the hip. We worked out together, went to church together, and spent most of our free time together. When I met Lynn's son, Murphy, I immediately thought he and my daughter Jimi would hit it off. But my matchmaking fell flat when, after meeting him, my free-spirited, hippie Jimi assured me he was "too preppy."

As winter turned into spring, Lynn invited me to her youngest son's baseball games. As a fan of the game (and Lynn's energy and contagious laughter), I accepted and was eager to cheer on Carter and my high school alma mater. After the first game, I was hooked and bought a season ticket to support the team. I felt calm sitting in the bleachers, and it was great to decompress after work.

Meeting Lynn certainly was a divine appointment. God gave us each other to walk through a season of singleness. Her invitation to a baseball game changed the course of my life forever. The boy who wasn't at all the type for my daughter became my son-in-law, and I received the precious gift of a granddaughter. Jimi and Murphy are amazing together, shining the light of Jesus to their generation through serving in the youth ministry at their church. They are marvelous parents to sweet Willow. Lynn and I are connected forever—as friends, in-laws, and grandmothers.

I love the good gifts He sends me: new beginnings, new friends, and a newfound sense of purpose. He showers me with beautiful moments and even has a sense of humor. My sweet Willow and her playful giggles and precious kisses are like parachute drops from heaven. She makes me laugh and brings light to any cloudy day.

When I stop long enough and pay attention, God gives the best hugs. His arms reach through the people in my life. In the warmth of the sun around my shoulders, the feel of the sun on my face, and so many other ways, I feel His divine embrace. God extends miracles too. I have experienced them. He answers prayers (even though sometimes the answer is no) and loves with an everlasting love.

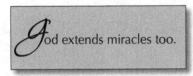

God extends miracles too.

God is relentless in His pursuit. My proof is that I was able to settle into a newness of life and go days without crying. Wearing a genuine smile—not a forced, fake "I'm fine" one—felt so awesome.

The things that were once ordinary, everyday activities became the very things that filled my soul. Previously taken for granted, now time with my children brought such joy. Conversations with dear friends were deeper and more intimate. Nearly every flower caught my eye. Even the pieces of driftwood on the sand brought awe, not indifference.

And the birds. Since that encounter with the sparrow at Starbucks, it seems my ears grew more attuned to their lofty melodies.

> Look at the birds of the air, for they neither sow nor reap nor gather into barns; yet your heavenly Father feeds them. Are you not of more value than they? (Matthew 6:26)

Sweet Friend,

God is good, and His plan is amazing and perfect. Even though there are times in life when it seems like all has been lost and there's wreckage everywhere, He is still beside you. The Savior sees every tear and wastes nothing. He loves you very much, and He is trustworthy.

I pray the healing Holy Spirit pours comfort and hope into your heart. Allow Him to be your safe place to land.

Let the Good Father of the universe repurpose your broken places.
Mer

—— IN HIS ARMS ——

People often ask others who are walking through a trial, "How do you cope?" or "I'm amazed at your strength. What keeps you so calm?" They may even ask, "How can you praise God in this tragedy?" Anytime someone asks me this type of question, I think of the poem I read and loved as a child. The poem is called "Footprints in the Sand" by Mary Stevenson. It was about a man who had a dream he was walking on the beach with the Lord. As they walked, scenes from his life flashed before him. During the display, he noticed that sometimes there were two set of footprints in the sand, and at other times there was only one set. This really bothered the man because it seemed that during the most difficult times, he only saw one set of footprints. So, he questions the Lord.

> "Why, when I needed you most,
> you have not been there for me?"
> The Lord replied,
> "The times when you have
> seen only one set of footprints,
> is when I carried you."

I can imagine the light going off in the man's mind at the Lord's reply. I certainly recognize the many moments that I never could have gotten through without the strength of the Father. Jesus carries those He loves. "The Lord is close to the brokenhearted and saves those who are crushed in spirit" (Psalm 34:18 NIV).

Hear Him whisper to your soul, "Child, I feel the pain of your heart right now."

Years after Lee's death, I had a coffee date with a friend whose husband had died suddenly at forty-four. Just two months after the loss, Amy was trying to figure out the day-to-day effort of getting through. She expressed the plethora emotions, specifically anger at God.

As Christians, we think it's taboo to admit we are angry at Him for allowing bad things to happen. When blame needs a scapegoat, God often is the target. It's okay. He understands human anger and can handle it; He loves us anyway. God isn't disappointed when His beloved children are confused. He is a patient father. He sticks close, and when the light bulb eventually comes on for us, God is complete in His forgiveness (Psalm 86:15). He always is generous with His grace.

Others who have not walked the path of pain don't get that grief has no limits. It's so personal that it's difficult to explain, even to the ones closest to us. And sometimes the most well-meaning people try to offer comforting words that hurt more than help. As Amy and I sat together, my mind went back to the moment I broke the silence of my own anger with God. It was a Sunday morning after church. As I drove home, the heat inside me started to rise, and before I had gone more than a mile, my distress turned into a full-blown ugly, sobbing cry. Anguish built and was released in a wail of frustration. I eventually pulled over to continue my rant. I beat the steering wheel and screamed at God, "Why would you do this to me? I am so mad at You!" As soon as those words came out of my mouth, I winced, even though I felt like God could have healed my mom and saved Lee.

As cars sped past, I felt a whisper in my heart say, "It's okay, I get you ... even in your anger." I looked across the table at Amy and smiled. She didn't know then that she eventually would be okay, but I did. I told her it was normal to be angry, hurt, and scared, because grief stinks. I knew one day she would laugh again and realize God had not done this *to* her, but that He had walked *with* her through it (Psalm 138:7). Amy simply needed someone to share her pain with—without expectations, without judgment, and without setting a timeline on her grief. She needed a friend to sit with her. These lyrics by Jason Gray express what my friend and many others try to say but don't know how: "While I wait for the smoke to clear, you don't even have to speak. Just sit with me in the ashes here, and together we can pray for peace to the One acquainted with our grief."

8

Morning Light

I will run and not grow weary,
I will walk, I will not faint.
I will soar on wings like eagles,
Find my rest in your everlasting name.
You are my revival,
Jesus on you I wait.
And I'll lean on your promise,
You will renew my strength.

—LAUREN DAIGLE, "MY REVIVAL"

"*Never give up on your dreams.*"

"Expect the unexpected."
"Never give up on your dreams."
"Miracles happen to those who believe in them."

These words of wisdom are easy to dismiss with an offhanded, "Whatever." But ask people who have suffered a tragedy, and they'll tell you about God's almighty power to change lives.

My friendship with Lynn led me to a ballpark, and the course of my life changed beyond my wildest dreams. Some friends had started asking me when I would be ready to date again, but I politely told them I wasn't at all interested and might never be. I'd always felt I was meant to be a wife, but my third time in a season of singleness felt right. I was content.

One afternoon while I was standing by the bleachers, an acquaintance of mine approached. And just like my first encounter with Lynn, the moment was another restart that happened in God's timing.

Jon Shave and I had attended the same high school and had run into each other occasionally over the years, but we'd never really known each other well. Yet one of the pros (or cons, depending on the situation) of living in a small town is that many people keep up with who's who and the juicy tidbits of each other's lives after graduation.

He had left Fernandina after high school to play college baseball and then was recruited by a professional team. After fifteen years, he returned to Fernandina and married, although it ended in divorce. Jon was single with two children.

When he walked up to me, I thought two things. *He's a nice guy, and he probably wants to get to know Lynn.* My dark-haired friend always turned heads. After making small talk for a few minutes, Jon walked away, and Lynn leaned over to me.

"Mer, I think he likes you." Apparently, I had been oblivious to his flirting.

"Huh? Nah, he was just coming over here to look at you."

Lynn assured me this wasn't the case. Jon didn't really have a reason to be at the ballpark, because his son was not old enough to play high school baseball. But he lived nearby and loved the game. Of course, I now know it was another divine appointment set by the Author of my life.

Later that night, I thought more about Jon. I remembered him as being shy and quiet, like my dad, and less like the men to whom I previously had been attracted. We talked more as the season progressed and we saw one another at the ballpark. Jon was refreshingly humble and sincere.

I was very attracted to him, but I was in a much different place emotionally and spiritually then I ever had been. I was not looking for a romantic relationship.

When Jon finally got up the nerve to ask me out, I was honest with him about my reservations. If he was looking for a rebound, for sex or adventurous drama, I was not the girl. My boring interests? Sitting at home and watching a movie or walking the beach. I kept waiting for his eyes to glaze over and for him to say, "Never mind."

"Okay, let's be friends and see where it goes," Jon said instead. "And if we only end up as friends, then we're friends."

Jon became my very best friend. Most mornings, he would come and pick me up, and as I took pictures of the sunrise, he would fish. Our dates were simple and comfortable, talking for hours and never allowing pretense to invade. We were up front and real with each other about every area of our lives, the good, the bad, and the ugly. He made me laugh, and better yet, he laughed at my jokes.

Not long after we started dating, I knew I could spend the rest of my life with this extraordinary man. Jon had a way about him. When I was with him, I felt like I was home. As our relationship grew more serious, I broke some news to him, wondering how he would respond. Once I explained what was on my heart, I think Jon was relieved.

> When I was with him, I felt like I was home.

As we talked, I explained to Jon that although I realized I had been so busy trying to feel loved in my previous relationships, I had forgotten my true love. I had gone from living in my parents' home to being a wife and mother. I had always had others to nurture and rescue, but I'd never allowed someone to rescue me. Throughout my first and second marriage, God always had been there, waiting for me to turn to Him, but I kept pushing Him to second or third place.

The Scripture says, "Nevertheless I have this against you, that you have left your first love" (Revelation 2:4). Throughout my life, I had put unrealistic expectations on others' natural love, assuming earthly love could fill my love tank and make me feel worthy. Only supernatural love can do that. The extravagant love of Jesus is enough. It fills, assigns worth, calms, heals, and restores.

Jesus had become my all in all, and so I told Jon that he could not be my first love. When Jesus held my head above the waves and carried me out of the treacherous water to the safety of the shore, He became my everything. He became my refuge and strength (Psalm 46); my rock, my fortress, and my deliverer (Psalm 18); and the one in whom I put all my trust (Psalm 91). The intimacy Christ offers is incomparable. There is so much freedom—freedom from fear (1 John 4:18), freedom from abandonment (Deuteronomy 31:6), and freedom from feeling unworthy.

Jon asked me to marry him after we had been dating about a year.

He was coaching baseball at the time, and so we casually agreed to wait until the season was over, which was late April. My mom had died on May 14, and Lee had died on May 16. We chose to get married on May 1, creating a happy start to what otherwise was a difficult month for me.

We decided on Wednesday to get married that Friday. I hadn't even thought about a dress, but a quick trip to one of our downtown shops delivered. I told the clerk I need a wedding dress to wear the next day. Without hesitating, she said she had the perfect dress.

And it was. It wasn't too fussy, it was knee-length, cream-colored, and sleeveless with a shear overlay that gave it just the right elegance. The ceremony was a small, quiet one with only a few family members by our side at our favorite spot on the beach. At sunrise, Jon and I pledged our forever love to each another and began the rest of our lives together.

Jesus was in His rightful place as my first love, and my love gauge read full. I was complete already, which meant so much freedom for Jon. He didn't take on the pressure of fulfilling my soul's desires. Jon was free to be himself, as well as my partner and helpmate in our marriage.

With Jon, God certainly blessed me beyond my imagination. Our blended family now also includes his children, Cisco and Katy, as well as Jon's mom, dad, and brother. I love them all and am constantly amazed at how the heart expands to hold so much affection and happiness.

Cisco, who just started college, is a quiet and very kind young man. He doesn't let things bother him but goes with the flow. I asked him one time why he doesn't get stressed about much. He replied, "I don't worry about stuff I can't control." A lot of wisdom for an eighteen-year-old.

Katy, eleven, sees the positive in most everything. One morning as she walked out of the front door, she noticed the sky was cloudy and growing darker. Her excitement bubbled over with, "Oh! It's going to rain. I think there will be a rainbow!" She's definitely a glass-half-full girl.

Jon's dad, Tommy, affectionately known as Papa, is a good man who is loving and wise. He always has a smile and a kiss on the cheek for me, and he makes me feel special. God even provided a mother when I didn't even realize I needed one. Jon's mom, Joyce, aka Mimi, is feisty and opinionated. She's passionate in the love she has for her children, grandchildren, and now me. We talk every morning on my way to work, on my way home, and whenever I need a mother's love and advice (which is often). When God does His work, He leaves no detail undone.

My children, Jimi and Bobby, are healthy young adults, having survived some hard situations and making difficult decisions. Over the years, I explained to both of them many times about the choice of being a victim or a victor, of living a life of excuses or pushing forward despite the past.

At twenty-seven, Jimi is an independent and fiercely loyal woman. She's a non-judgmental, people-loving disciple of Jesus, and she's an amazing wife and mother. Jimi has become my closest friend. Bobby is twenty-five and has more talent in his little finger than ten people put together. He is more reserved now compared to the extremely funny child who always had a hilarious remark growing up, however I still can see glimpses of my witty little boy. Bobby has a compassionate heart, and I see God doing an incredible work in his life. God has big plans for my son; I love watching it unfold.

I never will understand every twist and turn of my life on this side of heaven, but I do know the loving Father is patient and kind. He is the God of second (and third) chances. The joy I am experiencing as I walk through the rest of my life with Jon takes my breath away. Being his best friend, wife, and forever love feels so right. In fact, it feels like it has always been meant to be.

I often tell Jon I wish we had noticed each other in high school, fallen in love, and married, and that there always had been an us. In his wisdom, Jon smiles each time and says, "Darlin', God knew what He was doing. We might have messed it up way back then. His timing is perfect."

Jon is my blessing from the greatest and most gracious gift giver of all.

> By night on my bed I sought the one I love;
> I sought him, but I did not find him.
> 'I will rise now,' I said,
> 'And go about the city;
> In the streets and in the squares
> I will seek the one I love.'
> I sought him, but I did not find him.
> The watchmen who go about the city found me;
> I said, 'Have you seen the one I love?'
> Scarcely had I passed by them,
> When I found the one I love.
> I held him and would not let him go. (Song of Solomon 3:1–4)

Sweet Friend,

Do you think you'll never feel joy again? Let me assure you that although the night seems long, God always makes the sun rise. Kristene DiMarco of Bethel Music sings, "Take courage my heart, stay steadfast my soul, He's in the waiting, He's in the waiting. Hold onto your hope as your triumph unfolds, He's never failing, He's never failing."

God knows your deepest aches and all your soul's desires, and He cares. He is the precious Savior who tends to the brokenhearted, and He works out His good plan. Be thankful because God is faithful in His promises, and He never forsakes those He loves.

Keep your eyes on the hope of His horizon.
Mer

── Becoming a Butterfly ──

When I first accepted Christ into my heart as Lord and Savior, I surrendered my life to Him. As a new, on-fire Christian, there was an overwhelming sense of freedom. But as life moved forward, some days His freedom from temptation and sin felt less filling than my desire to please myself. It was hard to turn away from how I was used to living and turn toward what I knew to be right. Yet it is exactly what God called me to do.

Transitioning from one world into another is a difficult journey, much like becoming a disciple of Christ. The good news is that God does the changing. He leads; we follow.

As an example, Jon ate, worked, and slept baseball from childhood into adulthood. It was his entire life and was all he knew. When his career as a professional ballplayer ended, and he didn't wake up every day with that purpose, it was challenging for him physically, mentally, and socially. He felt out of place in so many ways. However, Jon kept looking forward and wanted to embrace the opportunities he hoped lay ahead.

This ability begins as soon as we look to the cross. In the Bible, Paul explains it this way: "Therefore, if anyone is in Christ, he is a new creation; old things have passed away; behold, all things have become new" (2 Corinthians 5:17).

In my mother's song, "Changed like a Butterfly," she compares the caterpillar's metamorphosis to a hell-bound life being born again as a new creation in Christ. The change is not without pain, however the result can only be described as amazing.

Living as a Christ follower is a transformation of heart and mind. "Do not conform to the pattern of this world, but be transformed by the renewing of your mind. Then you will be able to test and approve what God's will is—His good, pleasing and perfect will" (Romans 12:2 NIV).

Let's not be willing to settle for good, when God wants great for us. Although His perfect will doesn't always turn out how we expected, God longs to give us abundant life. Change is never easy, but it's always worth it. Just ask the caterpillar.

── Be Still, Trust Him ──

I often talk with Jon on the phone as he drives to work. One morning, I heard him exclaim, "Wait, little guy! Hey, Mer, I'll call you back." A few minutes later, Jon told me he'd seen a deer caught in a fence by the side of the road. He stopped to help, and the deer was able to free itself. The poor animal was totally panicked, but Jon shooed him away from the danger of traffic.

In my mind, I saw how it had played out: the fear of the deer and Jon's desire to rescue it. There have been times when, like the deer, I have been in total panic mode. I've gotten so focused on the crisis that I forget about the One who calms and saves. I often tell myself, "Hey, you're only human." But is that an excuse? Is it really the reason for the fear, or is it my unbelief?

I used to tell Jimi and Bobby when they were young, "Stop, look, and listen so that you don't have to stop, drop, and roll!" Similar advice for Christians is, "Be still, and know that I am God" (Psalm 46:10).

If the deer had only remained calm during its duress, it would have experienced the comfort of knowing someone bigger and stronger was there to help. It simply had to be still and trust. Jon's encounter with the deer reminded me how unpredictable life really is.

The choice is this: panic or trust? When I told a friend the story, she reminded me of the scripture that says, "The Lord will fight for you; you need only to be still" (Exodus 14:14 NIV).

Not long after we married, Jon took a new job that required him to travel. I freaked out during his first trip. I was so full of fear, worrying he might not come back alive (just like Lee), that I became physically ill. I tried to hide my panic from him when he called to check in, but Jon already knew me well enough to know I was struggling. He reassured me that God was in control and that everything was going to be fine. He called me often, and finally the three-day trip ended; he returned home.

Around his fifth trip, I began to relax and was able see what God was up to. The heavenly Father loves me so much that He was allowing me to heal from post-traumatic stress. Jon's traveling gave me the opportunity to work through fears I hadn't even realized I was harboring. I would like to say I never had another worry and was completely healed, however I'm still growing.

Life is the long process of becoming whole in Christ. Every time fear creeps in or total panic attempts to take over and paralyze, remember to take a deep breath and just be still.

Allow God to bring peace and direct those next steps. Take Him up on His promise to fight for good. He's trustworthy.

Nothing. Nada. Zip.

During the process of writing this book, I sat down a few different times at my keyboard, and no words came to mind. Not good. I had always enjoyed journaling, and writing during those times was like a God-fountain of words almost effortlessly flowing from my heart to my fingers. I clicked away until my fingers cramped.

These new blank-slate moments were frustrating. I chatted with God and reminded Him that I was doing this for Him. Still, zilch. I questioned whether I should be trying to write a book at all. *What if I fail? What if it's terrible, and no one wants to read it?* I quickly identified Satan as the author of these doubts.

Then, the soft whisper came. "I am your muse. Aren't you doing this with Me and for Me?"

The Spirit followed with this reminder, "Be strong and take heart and wait for the Lord" (Psalm 27:14 NIV).

I had tried to charge ahead, forgetting the only audience that mattered: my audience of One. God sees the motive of the heart, no matter how good the intention may be. The world of writer's block, the land of nothingness, is a scary place. But it got my attention and prompted me to look Godward instead of inward and how the world might judge me.

Desert places are times of waiting and feeling fruitless. The wilderness is where God does His most meaningful work. Faithfulness during days of drought gets rewarded. He pours His Spirit into thirsty souls, proving He is willing and able to do great things.

God is still good through writer's block. He is almighty when we are running through fields of flowers and when we feel stranded in the desert places of our lives. He teaches and has purpose in every season.

The focus and hope in all things is God, not self. He is the inspiration, the resolve, and the stamina.

> But those who wait on the Lord Shall renew their strength; They shall mount up with wings like eagles, They shall; run and not be weary, They shall walk and not faint. (Isaiah 40:31)

Tidal Waves, Tributaries, and Treasures

Sweet Friend,

When I get out of bed before dawn and go down to the beach with my camera in hand, I am hoping to catch a beautiful sunrise. On relatively calm mornings, I wade out as far as I deem safe, sometimes waste deep, and wait.

Hope. The dictionary defines it as "a feeling of expectation or desire for a certain thing to happen." (Of course, most mornings I hope there are no sharks scouting for their breakfast!) On a day-to-day basis, I think most people's earthly desire is to live a life of contentment with minimal stress and avoid pain. But when the ocean begins to get turbulent, often hope is lost.

Sometimes I have to remind myself that hope has nothing to do with the absence of trouble but everything to do with a relationship with Jesus, the Savior of our fallen world. He is the hope when storms come. Choosing to see the goodness of God, even in the most tragic situations, brings the remarkable realization that He is the lifeline to peace.

Perhaps you just have been hit by a tidal wave, that unexpected blow that knocks your feet out from under you, and now you're trying to catch your breath. Or you may be wading through a tributary in a season of waiting and searching. Maybe you are sifting through the memories of both, like sand falling through your fingers, and recalling the treasures provided along the way. No matter where you are on your life journey, God is with you and for you.

The Apostle Paul writes,

> *And we boast in the hope of the glory of God. Not only so, but we also glory in our sufferings, because we know that suffering produces perseverance; perseverance, character; and character, hope. And hope does not put us to shame, because God's love has been poured out into our hearts through the Holy Spirit, who has been given to us. (Romans 5:2–5 NIV)*

Don't lose heart, friend. God has a good plan for your life that is full of hope. His name is Jesus. He is steadfast in every season, He wants to walk with you through each one, and His hope is on the horizon.

As I continue to praise God in every sunrise, I know there will be more trials and sadness in my life. God doesn't promise a pain-free journey to heaven, but He does promise His presence and His strength to get through anything. And through the death of His Son on the cross, He promises an eternal home in Heaven for those who accept that sacrificial gift. In the words of the late Billy Graham, "My home is in Heaven. I'm just traveling through this world."

Thank you for reading my story. I pray that in some way, it has offered encouragement to press on. The next portion of this book is a compilation of thoughts or devotions I have written throughout the years. Please read through them in any way your spirit is stirred.

Allow God's waves of grace to wash over you as He wraps you in His love.

Love,
Mer

—— God's Tapestry ——

Have you ever looked at the backside of a section of tapestry while the artist is still working? It looks like a mish-mash of colorful lines. Not until the last thread is woven in can the beauty of the completed work be appreciated, and generally from a bit of a distance.

A child feels despondent when the sandcastle, nearly complete at the edge of the water, gets flooded and parts are washed away with the tide. Dad can envision the finished product, but for the child, it's disappointing.

Life often feels this way. When struggle, heartache, and tragedy are woven into our lives, it's difficult not to focus on anything but the immediate mess. God's Word promises, "Being confident of this very thing, that He who has begun a good work in you will complete it until the day of Jesus Christ" (Philippians 1:6).

The Master Weaver, the Great Architect, wants His very best for us. In the middle of the chaos, we forget to look at the Creator.

Accepting that God is working all things for good is a matter of trust. The seemingly tangled threads of our lives at a certain time may be what turn into a pattern of purpose. As others look on at what we see as a flattened heap of nothing, God could be revealing His steadfast faithfulness. And though we may never know this side of Heaven those who've watched us prevail as overcomers, God uses our lives to bring precious souls to the saving knowledge of Jesus.

Turn your eyes from what is temporal to what is eternal, from what's only for a brief season in this earthly life to what will endure through the ages, and fulfill the Almighty's purpose.

Consider these words: "While we do not look at the things which are seen, but at the things which are not seen. For the things which are seen are temporary, but the things which are not seen are eternal" (2 Corinthians 4:18).

Take a deep breath. If you are sitting on the beach and reading this, maybe wiggle your toes deeper into the sand and whisper, "I trust you, Jesus." God may not answer every why, but maybe, just maybe, He will allow you to catch a glimpse of His beautiful design, His tapestry of love.

There's a silly folktale about a fear-filled fowl. While Chicken Little is taking her morning walk, an acorn falls on her head, and she immediately thinks worst-case scenario. She starts telling all of her friends, "The sky is falling!" In other words, the world as she knew it was coming to an end.

Her friends believe her. Chicken Little, Henny Penny, Ducky Lucky, Turkey Lurkey, and Goosey Loosey are in an all-out panic. Their anxiety is through the roof, and they are not thinking clearly, which makes them a perfect target to fall prey to the enemy. Sly ol' Foxy Loxy, acting concerned and seemingly having all of the answers, offers to point them in the right direction ... or so they think. "Run into my den," he says. "You will be safe there while I go tell the king." Then, Foxy Loxy eats them all!

I never liked that story. I mean, really? Overreacting because of an acorn? How dumb.

Oh, wait. I have been a catastrophic thinker from time to time, focusing on all the what-if, worst-case scenarios. I've used so much energy worrying about something that never came to be or was totally insignificant. I have allowed so much anxiety into my heart and mind that I momentarily forgot I have a mighty warrior, God, on my side. He is for me and with me.

Irrational catastrophic thinking is never good. Truth is best. "Fear not, for I am with you; be not dismayed, for I am your God. I will strengthen you, yes, I will help you, I will uphold you with My righteous right hand" (Isaiah 41:10).

Too bad no one shared Apostle Peter's warning with Chicken Little. "Be sober, be vigilant; because your adversary the devil walks about like a roaring lion, seeking whom he may devour" (1 Peter 5:8). Satan, the opportunist, is looking for any occasion to trip us up. Being sober (clearheaded) and vigilant (keeping careful watch for possible danger or difficulties) is our defense against his attack.

When panic begins to tighten in our chests, we must take a deep breath and remember the truth. "For God has not given us a spirit of fear, but of power and of love and of a sound mind" (2 Timothy 1:7).

The Savior is completely trustworthy. When it seems like the sky is falling, run to Jesus for the calm reassurance that everything will be all right.

—— PERSEVERANCE ——

One late afternoon, my daughter, Jimi, and I were strolling through Fernandina's historic downtown. We saw what I thought was an amazing sight. A beautiful purple flower was growing up through a crack in the base of a hundred-year-old brick building. I don't know the type of flower, but I named her Perseverance.

Precious little Perseverance had grown in the most unlikely of places. Against all odds, she had bloomed right where the Creator had put her.

At the very beginning of this book (chapter 1, "Walk with Me"), I include the lyrics of a song by Plumb: "How many times have you heard me cry out, 'God please take this?' How many times have you given me strength to just keep breathing?" Oh, how those words resonate! We beg God to relieve our pain, and instead He helps us survive the trial.

The Bible instructs us to "be joyful in hope, patient in affliction, faithful in prayer" (Romans 12:12 NIV). From my experiences, I believe God is more concerned with the development of our character than our comfort. Miss Perseverance surely didn't find it easy or comfortable flourishing between brick and concrete, but it was the only way she could live in total dependence on the Maker and grow to her full potential. I like to think God simply put her there just for me, as a reminder of His love.

The Apostle Paul, who wrote many of the New Testament letters from prison, testified, "I served the Lord with great humility and with tears and in the midst of severe testing" (Acts 20:19 NIV). We too are called to endure with patience and hope.

The next time you're in a tight spot or are weary from difficulty, remember the purple flower growing up through a crack, and keep pushing forward. Persevere and show others that they can too.

The bad news: We're in the midst of a battle.

The good news: We have a warrior God.

Is the struggle an illness, a failing marriage, a wayward child? Maybe it's fighting against fear, grief, or depression. The Merriam-Webster dictionary defines a battle as "a combat between two persons, to fight or struggle tenaciously to achieve or resist something."

Scripture confirms, "For our struggle is not against flesh and blood, but against the rulers, against the authorities, against the powers of this dark world and against the spiritual forces of evil in the heavenly realms" (Ephesians 6:12 NIV). Spiritual warfare is real. Satan wants souls, and he uses feelings and emotions like shame, loneliness, and unworthiness. He's cunning. In fact, he "walks about like a roaring lion, seeking whom he may devour" (1 Peter 5:8).

But we have a God who is victorious. He is the light that shines in the darkness, and it cannot be overcome. Our God is personal. He fights for and with, us. "But the Lord is with me like a mighty warrior; so my persecutors will stumble and not prevail. They will fail and be thoroughly disgraced; their dishonor will never be forgotten" (Jeremiah 20:11 NIV).

One of my very favorite reminders of God's greatness is found in 2 Samuel, when David inquires of God regarding an upcoming battle. God tells him, "As soon as you hear the sound of marching in the tops of the poplar trees, move quickly, because that will mean the Lord has gone out in front of you to strike the Philistine army" (2 Samuel 5:24 NIV). David was obedient and waited for the signal, even though he was a man of action and war. I'm almost certain waiting was not his forte, but David had learned over time, from one battle to another, about God's faithfulness to His promises. Obedience equals victory.

God's victory is our victory! "If God is for us, who can be against us?" (Romans 8:31) God knows our struggles, and He cares. If we can be still and calm our breathing, tilting our ears toward the sound, we will hear the marching of the celestial army arriving to win the battle.

Believe. Trust. Be faithful and wait on the Lord.

Know God and embrace His victory.

⸺ The Key ⸺

Trying to unlock a door with the wrong key is frustrating. And it's futile, to say the least.

Often it is obvious because it won't even fit in the keyhole. But then there are the keys that fit well and simply will not unlock the door. No matter how much we jiggle it, it's the wrong key.

The door to life, with its many twists and turns, requires the correct key as well. I didn't write *keys* plural, but the singular *key*. There is only one key to get through this life and into the eternal kingdom. His name is Jesus. "Jesus said to him, 'I am the way, the truth, and the life. No one comes to the Father except through Me'" (John 14:6).

God knows we struggle with accepting that Jesus is the only answer to every question. He strategically reminds again and again that His ways are better than our ways. "Trust in the Lord with all your heart, and lean not on your own understanding; in all your ways acknowledge Him, and He shall direct your paths" (Proverbs 3:5–6). We do not have other choices. There are no alternatives, just Jesus. We make it hard, but really it is so simple.

Perhaps a bigger house or a vacation will fix the marriage. A night out with friends and a few drinks certainly will make the loneliness go away. I picture people walking around like the janitor with a hundred different keys, trying each one, when all that's needed is the one key. Such a collection of fake keys is heavy and weighs us down; they cause confusion.

It's time to lighten the load. Throw away all the other keys except for the master key. Don't call the local locksmith. Reach for the One who works perfectly every single time. Jesus is all we need.

Empowered

I read some very sad words in Lisa Bevere's book, *Lioness Arising*. The author wrote, "Because of fear, I had forfeited strength, life and beauty. I had lost a sense of my true self and, with that loss, so much of what God wanted for me was yet unrealized."

Fear certainly has a way of keeping us from realizing all God has for us. As women, we sometimes want to put a finger to the chest of this world and scream, "I am woman. Hear me roar!" Yet we're scared inside. We wear our game faces and then wait for the world to tell us we are not worthy, not part of the in crowd, or not a good wife, mother, friend, or co-worker.

It's no wonder that *empowered* is a buzzword among women. The dictionary gives this definition: "give (someone) the authority or power to do something, make (someone) stronger and more confident, especially in controlling their life and claiming their rights." We desire to be liberated, not shackled by our fear of failure, rejection, and other's opinions. Yet we can't seem to break out of the bondage of self-depreciation.

Studying God's Word together as sisters in Christ is a tool to freedom. "And He said to me, 'My grace is sufficient for you, for My strength is made perfect in weakness'" (2 Corinthians 12:9). The Apostle John lovingly tells us, "You are of God, little children, and have overcome them, because He who is in you is greater than he who is in the world" (1 John 4:4).

We are cherished, loved, favored, treasured, and precious. We are worth dying for and staying for, beloved and empowered. It's not because of the balance in our bank accounts, the brands we wear, or the crowd we hang with. It's not because of who we are but because of *whose* we are and *whose* strength is in us.

Chin up, shoulders back! We must claim our rightful place. We are daughters of the King of kings!

── Come Home ──

I remember my children singing songs about Jesus when they were young and coming home from Sunday school with Bible verses memorized. Innocence abounded. I never thought they one day would go down a wayward path ... but they did.

Thankfully, God pursued and drew them back to Him. The waiting was hard. As a mother, I did everything I could to make them see truth, but at the end of the day, they had to make their way back to the Father.

I love the parable Jesus tells about the prodigal son. The youngest boy wanted his inheritance early, and when he received it, he left home and spent all of it on "riotous living" (Luke 15:13). Leaving the protection of his father's house in order to follow his own desires, the son lived it up and did what he wanted to do. When he hit rock bottom, he returned home with intentions to humble himself and be a servant in his father's house.

Then comes my favorite part: "And he arose, and came to his father. But when he was yet a great way off, his father saw him, and had compassion, and ran, and fell on his neck, and kissed him" (Luke 15:20). I love the middle part the most. "But when he was yet a great way off, his father saw him." This tells me the father knew his child well and was watching with expectancy for his return.

Waiting. Watching. The father had gone about his daily routine, all the while watching for his precious child to come home. It didn't matter how many months or years the son was gone; the father never stopped looking down the road that led to home.

Like the prodigal son's father, we have the faithful, heavenly Father who loves us even in our wandering. My daddy would say, "When you feel like God has abandoned you, Meredith, turn around. He didn't move—you did. God is the same yesterday, today, and forever."

Poor choices, detours, and even pigpens don't mean the end. God's love is unconditional and everlasting. He is the compassionate Father and does not lay on guilt trips or say, "I told you so."

"Then I will give them a heart to know Me, that I am the Lord; and they shall be My people, and I will be their God, for they shall return to Me with their whole heart" (Jeremiah 24:7). The Father is watching with expectancy and waiting with open arms. Turn around and return home.

—— A Man of Sorrows ——

In a week's time, a friend of mine was diagnosed with cancer. Another had a miscarriage, losing the precious baby she and her husband had been waiting on for over two years. Yet another friend's husband went to heaven after a long battle with brain cancer. All these dear ones grieved, and most likely they grieved differently.

One of the many beautiful attributes of the good Father is the way He loves us right where we are. When we are crushed beneath the wave of sorrow, He loves us there. When we are screaming the anguish of "Why?" He loves us there. Even when we turn our back to His comfort, He loves us and is patiently waiting for us to turn again into His faithful arms.

I love the many reminders in scripture. "Even though I walk through the valley of the shadow of death, I will fear no evil: for thou art with me; thy rod and thy staff they comfort me" (Psalm 23:4). "And the Lord, He is the One who goes before you. He will be with you, He will not leave you nor forsake you; do not fear nor be dismayed" (Deuteronomy 31:8). These verses gently whisper to our hurting hearts that our loving God is with us through every tear, every anxiety attack, every fit of anger, every fragmented prayer, and every effort just to breathe. He holds us in His arms when we can't walk, and He stands beside us, holding our hand when we start taking those baby steps out of the valley of despair.

While going through a trial or tragedy, often well-meaning people offer, "I know how you feel." But everyone deals with grief differently; a more accurate sentiment may be, "I don't know exactly what you are going through, but my heart hurts for you and I am praying for you."

Jesus is the only one who can understand entirely what we are feeling and how we hurt. "He is despised and rejected by men, a Man of sorrows and acquainted with grief. And we hid, as it were, our faces from Him; He was despised, and we did not esteem Him. Surely He has borne our grief and carried our sorrows" (Isaiah 53:3–4). There is no suffering Jesus the man, or God the Father has not faced.

We must not be ashamed of how we are feeling while walking through a dark valley, because Abba Father already has been there ahead of us, and He doesn't leave us to face it alone. It may be hard to see in the midst of sadness, but there is a comforter and a light in the darkness.

There is an exquisite artist who creates "beauty from ashes." His name is Jesus.

—— Be the Door ——

You know by now that music inspires me. I like rhythm, but I'm a lyric listener. As a child, when a song came on the radio, I would say, "Momma, listen to these words."

Jason Gray's "With Every Act of Love" includes a line that says, "God put a million, million doors in the world for His love to walk through and one of those doors is you." Many songs are inspired by God's Word, and we who are created in His image are meant to worship Him and point others to Him.

"He who does not love does not know God, for God is love" (1 John 4:8). Do we ooze the love that resides in us? Are we a door, or even just a welcome mat, to His kingdom for everyone with whom we work and play?

Consider a room filled with vases of gardenias or roses—the pleasant aroma fills every corner. The same is true for us: whatever we fill ourselves with the most will pour out of our mouths and show in our actions (2 Corinthians 2:15).

Minds and hearts filled with Jesus radiate love. Spending time in the Bible and praying for God to use us helps us to be on the lookout for opportunities to be the hands and feet of Christ. We'll also see others through the eyes of Christ. We will love with no agenda, no self-driven motive and no expectation of a payback.

Holy obedience opens up opportunity for an abundant harvest of souls. We share God's love and He does the rest. Let's be gentle, kind, cheerful, and encouraging. Helpers and compassionate listeners. Let's be doors.

—— Known by God ——

Oftentimes words and phrases nearly jump off pages and beg for my attention.

Recently, while reading the book of Ruth, I noticed something new. Naomi forgot who she was. After her husband and two sons die, she and her daughter-in-law Ruth returned to Naomi's hometown. When people recognized her as she entered the gate, she told them to no longer call her Naomi, but to refer to her as Mara, which means "bitter" (Ruth 1:20).

I sat in the sorrow she must have experienced. She told her friends, "I went out full, and the Lord has brought me home again empty." She was understandably focusing on her loss.

As I kept reading, I was intrigued. The author, most likely Samuel, never stopped referring to her as Naomi. The inspired Word of God continued to call her by her given name, not her self-proclaimed one! Renaming ourselves by our current state of mind does not accurately define who we are in Christ. He always sees us through the eyes of His unchanging love.

Life is unpredictable. Plans change and life can take unexpected twists and turns. It may even resemble Kingda Ka at Six Flags (the scariest roller coaster in the world), but we have a dependable God. When tempted to exist only as anger, bitterness, broken, hatefulness, failure, unworthy, or unwanted, we must stop and remember *whose* we are.

The loving Father wraps His arms around every broken heart, every broken life, and whispers, "You are My precious daughter, you are My greatly loved son; I see your situation and haven't forgotten you." Even when we try to change our names due to temporary memory lapse, rest assured that we are known by God.

Soak in the comforting words from the Redeemer: "Fear not, for I have redeemed you; I have called you by your name; you are Mine" (Isaiah 43:1).

Shark's Teeth

I remember a time when I was trying to figure out God's will for my life. It seemed as elusive as finding a shark's tooth on the beach. I searched and searched, and I even thought I found one. But it wasn't a shark's tooth at all; upon closer inspection, it was only a broken shell, a counterfeit. Sometimes we feel like we're looking in the right places and heading in the right direction, certain the path we're on is God's will. Then a look in the mirror reveals more self-serving intentions than selflessness. I have made decisions based on what I wanted and then tried to justify my actions by claiming God's will. But they were my own selfish desires—broken pieces trying to look like something genuine and valuable. Maybe we make it too hard. We want so badly for God's will to match our agenda that we pick up anything that's shiny, but all He really wants from us is our devotion. If our purpose as Christ followers is to worship Him and build His kingdom, then the particular path we walk is not as imperative as the way we walk it. Maybe it isn't in all the tiny details. The often quoted scripture "For I know the plans I have for you ... plans to prosper you and not to harm you, plans to give you hope and a future" (Jeremiah 29:11NIV) entices us to think God wants to pave the road we travel here on earth with gold. Jesus actually is talking about our salvation, our eternal life with Him.

Instead of desperately trying to discover what we believe is His will for us, why don't we desperately seek Him? We can worship and serve God in any city or job.

He vows, "You will seek Me and find Me, when you search for Me with all your heart" (Jeremiah 29:13). Eyes open to the possibilities will find the true treasure.

—— Pedicure Therapy ——

One morning at therapy—actually, I was getting a pedicure (which *is* therapy!)—my friend and pedicurist Rhonda and I were talking about life and dysfunction. For years over a spa tub and nail polish, she and I have dug deeper, well beyond the normal salon chitchat.

That morning we were talking about how we think God allows tribulations so that His children don't get too comfortable here on this earth. Many are merely existing, paralyzed by uncertainty, rather than living with expectancy of God's goodness and favor.

We talked about Lee, and Rhonda told me how she thought others viewed our marriage. After hearing that they thought we had the absolute perfect marriage, I felt I needed to clear up some things. Lee was not perfect (and certainly I'm not either!), and our relationship was not without fault. Two flawed people doing life together isn't always butterflies and rainbows.

We tried to make the best of what we had to work with, and the only way we were able to maintain a healthy marriage was with God at the center. Lee would say, "Mer, I'm glad we are in this foxhole together, but we're only going to make it with Jesus in here with us!"

Jesus taught, "But seek first the kingdom of God and His righteousness, and all these things shall be added to you" (Matthew 6:33). Making God's will a priority in marriage helps to ensure sustainability. Relationships are where Satan likes to meddle. Two people can resist an attack, but with God in the circle of intimacy, the devil can't distract and destroy (Ecclesiastes 4:12).

Be careful not to underappreciate your mate in the mundane of the everyday. Don't compare your relationship to others. That's in Satan's toolbox too. Be vigilant to tell the people you care about that you treasure them. Don't make them guess.

Keep God where He longs to be: at the core of marriage. That way, love flourishes.

—— DNA ——

Oh, the intrigue. A TV commercial offered to use my DNA to reveal my heritage, and the possibility of knowing from where my ancestors came, and the different nationalities that could be embedded into my genetic makeup! Every time the commercial ran, the more I really wanted to know the history of my maternal grandmother's Native American tribe. Imagine my delight when my mother-in-law gave me a DNA kit for my birthday.

It's amazing the things science can discover. All this information at my fingertips from just a small amount of saliva? I followed the directions with precision and mailed in my DNA with excitement. Waiting for the results certainly was a lesson in patience. When the data arrived, revealing I am less than 1 percent Native American, I was sorely disappointed. My entire life, I truly had believed I was part American Indian.

Instead, I found out that I am Irish, Scottish, Welsh, German, and Scandinavian; I even have some Russian thrown into the mix. If anyone asked, I told myself, it may be less confusing to say, "I'm a little bit country and a little bit rock 'n' roll" (people my age will get it).

My Godly lineage (and yours too!) isn't confusing at all. It is exact, and there is no guessing as to my heritage. The Word tells me, "But as many as received Him, to them He gave the right to become children of God, to those who believe in His name" (John 1:12). Once we accept Christ as the Savior, the buck stops here, so to speak. We don't really need further instruction, but the words "I am the Alpha and the Omega, the Beginning and the End, the First and the Last" (Revelation 22:13) seal the case.

We no longer need to search through the ashes of time for our origin and the origin of our forefathers because once we belong to the household of faith, the family line begins and ends with the blood of Jesus.

As a child of the living God, I know who I am and *whose* I am. There's nothing wrong with curiosity as to earthly ancestry, but with Jesus, there's powerful confidence in claiming birthrights to the Eternal King.

— LAND OF BLAH —

A local church youth leader and dear friend recently shared that she was in a slump and feeling "kind of blah" about everything. She was discouraged and wondered whether she was doing enough for the teens God had placed in her life to nurture and guide.

As Christians, we have a desire to help others find the path to everlasting life. When that doesn't happen in our timing, we can feel not enough, like we are not making a difference or living up to expectations (often our own).

When my children were teenagers, my mother's heart wanted them to be happy. At the same time, I wanted them to make wise decisions and stay out of trouble. I prayed, spoke God's truth to them, nagged, and worried. Yet at the end of the day, who they were going to become and what they were going to stand for was their decision. As much as I tried to be their junior Holy Spirit, I was simply their mom. I had to trust God to do His work in their hearts.

Don't go thinking I'm a spiritual supermom! I released my kids into the hands of Jesus kicking and screaming. In one breath, I said I trusted Him to protect them, and in the next breath I practically curled up in the fetal position with worry.

Many seasons of life can feel like the land of blah: mothering little ones, when never getting out of the house is a constant; working fifty-plus hours a week, month after month; and wandering around an empty nest, silently grieving a lost purpose. The mundane certainly can seem purposeless.

But in God there is significance in every season (Ecclesiastes 3:1–8). We simply need to stay close and seek Him. When discouragement comes, take time to still the questions. Sit quietly with Him and repent, refocus, and regroup.

First, I ask God to reveal anything in my life that I need to repent of or dispose of so that I can be useful for His kingdom. Maybe I'm not trusting Him or His plan? Second, I refocus my attention on Jesus, my savior, refuge, and warrior. Perhaps I'm too focused on myself? Then, I regroup and remind myself, "You are a child of God. You belong to Him, and your life is for Him." I spend time in prayer and then meditate on

Paul's words: "I press toward the goal for the prize of the upward call of God in Christ Jesus" (Philippians 3:14).

Shine His light in every season and every place. Trust and pray for loved ones and friends, encouraging and speaking truth with grace. Be available, be expectant, and be ready.

Stand back and watch as Jesus illuminates souls!

──── Bend Your Knees ────

Pulling a muscle often happens unexpectedly. Move the wrong way or don't lift properly—and ouch! A muscle strain is painful and often inconvenient. When I strain a muscle at the gym, it's usually because I haven't stretched enough or worked out consistently.

The same may happen to our spirits. If we aren't in the Word regularly and praying, we can easily get offended by others. Certainly there are times when someone says or does something intentionally, but many times it doesn't have anything to do with the offender. He or she may not even know feelings have been hurt.

When we're overly sensitive, likely there's something much deeper going on inside. Often the offense really isn't worth getting our feathers ruffled or allowing it to distract us from our walk with Christ. I once had a friend who would say, "I just let things go, like water off a duck's back." He didn't obsess over little annoyances and kept smiling.

But that isn't as easy as it sounds for some. Ultrasensitive people have tender spirits, and asking God for a confidence boost and to fortify the spirit is important. His strength is the answer.

Satan tries to steal our joy with offenses. Jesus warns, "The thief does not come except to steal, and to kill, and to destroy. I have come that they may have life, and that they may have it more abundantly" (John 10:10). When insults sting, look to Jesus.

The rule of thumb for heavy lifting is to "bend your knees and lift with your legs." The same goes for dealing with life's offences. If we bend our knees in prayer and give it to God, we can get up and walk confidently the path set before us.

Consider the lies and betrayals Jesus endured in order to give us the ultimate abundant life. He knew His truth and was sustained by His purpose to fulfill the Father's plan. We must do the same.

—— GOD-SIZE DREAM ——

What were your childhood fantasies? Whom did you aspire to be when you grew up?

When I was thirteen, I was certain I would be a successful jockey, riding in the Kentucky Derby. In high school, I dreamed of traveling the world as a National Geographic photographer. Neither of those ever came to fruition, and at twenty-one, I was a wife, a mother, and a fulltime bank employee.

I'm not saying children's dreams are silly or their aspirations are never fulfilled—look at all the Olympic athletes—but often the ideas we have for our future are shortsighted. God's plans, on the other hand, are good and perfect. "In their hearts, humans plan their course, but the Lord establishes their steps" (Proverbs 16:9 NIV).

Although math has never been my thing, I am still in mortgage banking twenty-seven years later. As I reflect on my life, I know my job doesn't define me, and my work rarely is about numbers. The relationships far outweigh the worksheets and closing documents. God has put me in a place to help people and be His mouthpiece; He knew my sweet spot wasn't on the back of a horse or behind a camera in some faraway land, but rather face-to-face with those He wants to reach.

As a mother, I had dreams for my young children as they grew into teenagers. The potential I saw in certain areas of their life lured me to map out in my mind possible career paths for them. When Jimi was a freshman in high school, she could argue so well and convincingly that I was sure she would be a powerful lawyer one day. I had Bobby ready to be a Major League Baseball prospect when he was seven. But even the most elaborate dreams we parents have for our children cannot compare to the Father's dream for them. The world's view of our children's accomplishments is about how popular they are and how much money they will make someday. God sees how much like Himself they are becoming.

In ancient times, the shepherd boy David dreamed only of leading and protecting his sheep. However, God saw a king of nations and a "man after His own heart." Joseph dreamed that he would rule over his brothers one day. That paled in comparison to God's plan: ruling over all of Egypt, which included saving his family and an entire generation from starvation. Mary was looking forward to being a wife and someday a mother, but God asked her to give birth to and raise His Son.

The Sovereign One is a game-changing God. No matter what we dream up for ourselves, He has an even better plan. Let Him dream for you!

── ONE TRUE SELF ──

While I was growing up, especially during my teen years, my mother occasionally would quote Shakespeare: "To thine own self be true." The first time I heard it, I asked her what it meant. In *Hamlet*, Polonius, the advisor to the king and father to Laertes, gave his son this advice as he was leaving on a trip.

Mom explained it was a reminder to Laertes that even though he would be away from home, he should always remember who he was inside and should live a good and noble life. Then she told me that she and Dad had done their best to instill in their girls the truths of faith, but it was up to us to embrace those truths and decide whose we are. Needless to say, when I often faced temptation, I heard my mother's voice in my head saying, "Meredith, remember whose daughter you are, and to thine own self be true."

As the years passed, I appreciated my mother's wisdom. But as I became more acquainted with Scripture, I struggled with the philosophy of the old adage. In fact, the New Testament says, "I have been crucified with Christ and I no longer live, but Christ lives in me. The life I now live in the body, I live by faith in the Son of God, who loved me and gave Himself for me" (Galatians 2:20 NIV). Also, Jesus declares, "Then He said to them all, 'If anyone desires to come after Me, let him deny himself, and take up his cross daily, and follow Me'" (Luke 9:23).

We are to die to self. I wondered, *Could Mom have been wrong?* She was a godly and wise woman, and I was certain my mom would have thought this advice through and measured it against God's Word before imparting it to her children.

Deciding to try to think like Jimi Buck, I searched the Scripture some more. "For in Him we live and move and have our being" (Acts 17:28). Also, "But he who is joined to the Lord is one spirit with Him" (1 Corinthians 6:17).

Being true to ourselves is being true to Christ. We are made in the image of the one true, holy God, and the Spirit of truth lives in us to keep us from all temptation and evil.

I concluded my mom was giving us biblical wisdom. We are one with Christ and indwelled with the Holy Spirit so that we can confidently heed, "To thine own self be true."

—— GNATS ——

Those irritating little creatures! Biting gnats, or swarms of no-see-ums, as we call them in the South, are pesky and downright distracting. The teeny, tiny things buzz around ears and bite like crazy.

These pests certainly can be a distraction from doing the work of the Lord, particularly mission work outdoors. But what about the spiritual pests on our everyday faith walk? The annoying co-worker, the rude clerk, the inconvenient car breakdown, the bad hair day, the sarcastic friend. They're not major disturbances, to be sure, but people and situations can sting our spirits. Such annoyances can veer us off course, make us cranky, and cause us to miss opportunities to minister to others.

Jesus affirms living this earthly life isn't easy; it means "tribulation" (John 16:33). Satan loves to mess with our marriages, friend circles, and daily agendas. He probably mutters to himself, "I can't have her soul, but I can bug (no pun intended!) the living daylights out of her and make her feel like she isn't any good to God."

How do we stand firm against this evil? "For God has not given us a spirit of fear, but of power and of love and of a sound mind" (2 Timothy 1:7). The Holy Spirit is our inner safeguard.

Like bug spray, we're instructed in Ephesians how to repel Satan. "Finally, be strong in the Lord and in His mighty power. Put on the full armor of God, so that you can take your stand against the devil's schemes" (Ephesians 6:10–11 NIV). Additional verses describe that "mighty" as "the belt of truth," "the breastplate of righteousness," "the shield of faith," "the helmet of salvation" and "the sword of the Spirit."

When gnats try to swarm our faith, we must swat them away with the goodness, faithfulness, and power of God. Instead of becoming preoccupied with all the little frustrations in life, let's praise God for our blessings, allowing the annoyances to blow away on the breeze of His grace.

—— Come Alive ——

I woke up one morning with a song in my head. *(Thankfully, it wasn't "We all live in a yellow submarine ...")* The chorus of "Come Alive (Dry Bones)" by Lauren Daigle kept repeating in my mind and flowing from my lips as I went about my morning.

> As we call out to dry bones
> Come alive, come alive
> We call out to dead hearts
> Come alive, come alive
> Up out of the ashes
> Let us see an army rise
> We call out to dry bones, come alive

I was overwhelmed by the absolute power of God. I thought to myself, *Wow, there have been so many times the Holy Spirit has renewed me and brought me back to life. I am so thankful.* Then it occurred to me, this is about so much more than just my renewal. It's about the one and only miraculous power.

I was compelled to open my Bible and read about how God set Ezekiel in a valley with an army of dead people. They were not only vast, but the bones were "very dry," meaning the men had been dead a long time. God asked Ezekiel, "Son of man, can these bones live?" Ezekiel answered, "O Lord God, You know" (Ezekiel 37:3).

The Holy Spirit reminded me, just as He may have reminded Ezekiel, that with us things may seem impossible, but with God anything is possible. I wept with relief.

Ezekiel knew the God he served and obeyed was a God of hope in hopeless situations. He relayed the message from God to the piles of bones, telling them God would cause breath to enter them, and they would live; He would restore flesh over the bones, and they would know He was the Lord.

Today, as disciples of Christ, we are called to proclaim the message that God can save and has the power to breathe life into dead things. We are to be obedient and share the gospel ... and then stand by and watch as the Holy Spirit breathes everlasting life into hearts once dead.

As a former corpse myself, I can attest that nothing is too difficult for God.

—— Peeling Eggs ——

Most mornings, I boil eggs for my two co-workers and myself. Sometimes the eggs peel with ease, the shell and skin seeming to slip right off. But other times I'm tempted to throw the egg in the trash for all the frustration and trouble it causes.

Life is like that. Some days and weeks are easy, dreamlike almost, and we feel like we're walking on clouds. Then other times, everything is more complicated. Our families or our jobs are like the uncooperative eggshell that sticks to the tender egg white.

"For He makes His sun rise on the evil and on the good, and sends rain on the just and on the unjust" (Matthew 5:45). Being a Christ follower doesn't protect us from the yuck in life. It's what we do with the unpleasant or downright horrible days that make a difference.

We have a choice: scream, throw a fit, and toss the proverbial egg in the trash, or remember it's just life. "This is the day the Lord has made; we will rejoice and be glad in it" (Psalm 118:24). It's really a matter of perspective and purpose. There is good in the midst of bad, and difficult times often are when our character is developed and we grow. We must fill our minds and hearts with God's Word (His love letter to us) and lean into His will.

God doesn't leave us without a reprieve. Jesus invites, "Come to Me, all you who labor and are heavy laden, and I will give you rest" (Matthew 11:28).

My mother would say, "Darling, this too shall pass." No matter how messed up the day may seem, even if the egg white is demolished, remember that there's always the yoke, nourishment for survival.

God is the God of both great days and horrible eggshell days. Chin up! God has a plan.

Go Organic

It seems a lot of people are going organic these days—fertilizer, food, cleaners, and even cookware. With such a desire to live chemical-, hormone-, synthetic-, GMO-, and BPA-free lives, we should also be choosing organic joy.

Wait, what? Organic joy is the difference between being happy for a time and living a truly joyful life. Let me explain. Although many people strive to be happy, their happiness may be full of synthetics. Perhaps they're seeking fulfillment through a relationship, their job, their wealth, their children, or even their social circle. These may bring moments of temporary external happiness, but true and lasting joy isn't found in any person or thing other than Christ.

It's easy to get caught up in the hype of creating our own happiness. Sadly, that never lasts. Happiness is circumstantial. The joy Jesus gives is internal and everlasting; it remains even when tragedy strikes. Joy is knowing there's always hope, always a reason to praise God. Speaking from experience, any other substitute leaves us in want.

Jesus said, "I am the true vine and My Father is the vinedresser" (John 15:1). Jesus goes on to give us the recipe for joy. He says, "Abide in Me, and I in you. As the branch cannot bear fruit of itself, unless it abides in the vine, neither can you, unless you abide in Me" (John 15:4). Then He puts a bow on it with, "These things I have spoken to you, that My joy may remain in you, and that your joy may be full" (John 15:11).

The main ingredient for lasting and true joy is to abide (obey, hold on) in the vine. It's a fruit (like love, peace, and self-control) that grows out of a life with Jesus (Galatians 5:22). Then it's passed on. Once we have the joy that comes from Christ, we want to share it with others. Much like when we start eating healthier and see the benefits.

Bottom line: True and lasting joy, the peace that surpasses all understanding, is the result of an intimate relationship with Christ. Oh, and it's free! Jesus already paid the exorbitant price for us when He died on the cross for our sins.

This is the real deal. No gimmicks, no hidden ingredients, no sleight of hand ... just Jesus. Pure "organic joy" can be found only in Christ. Don't wait. Go organic.

THE GOOD INVESTMENT

I had a dream one night that I'd made a good investment and came into a lot of money. In the dream, a friend hugged me the next day and said, "You don't feel any richer."

"That's because I was rich already. The other is just money." I woke up, and even though I was a little disappointed a windfall wasn't sitting in my bank account, I knew the dream was God's truth.

I am rich. God has blessed me abundantly. I may not have a large bankroll, but I have things money can't buy, and I am extremely thankful. The priceless gift of salvation is enough, and yet He has given me so much more: health; an amazing family and group of friends who are Christ followers; a precious, healthy granddaughter; a safe home; and a fulfilling job. I even count the trials in my life as blessings because those times grew my faith and trust in Christ.

Jesus teaches, "But lay up for yourselves treasures in heaven" (Matthew 6:20). Investing in earthly possessions brings only temporary happiness. Using our time, talent, and resources with a cheerful, generous heart for God's kingdom is eternal. Sometimes I feel a bit sad when I think about the early years with my children. I worked hard to make a living and provide for what we needed. Long hours at the bank meant missing out on moments I can never get back. There were times I was physically present but not mentally; —my mind was working a mortgage deal or worrying about clients' needs.

As a citizen of Heaven, the urgency of my loved ones requires my wholehearted devotion. Even though I cannot retrace my steps, I have learned that the "stop and drop everything" response to my family's needs (while still being responsible at work) pleases God. Paul wrote to the Christians in Corinth, reminding them, "But this I say: He who sows sparingly will also reap sparingly, and he who sows bountifully will also reap bountifully" (2 Corinthians 9:6).

Jesus often went out of His way, or stopped what He was doing, to help those in need. Consider the time Jesus took the road through Samaria to meet the woman at the well, or how He passed through Jericho and made time to dine with the tax collector Zacchaeus. He also pardoned the woman caught in the act of adultery, healed the bleeding woman in the crowd, and restored the sight of blind Bartimaeus. What if He had said, "I'm too busy with my ministry to help these people"?

Sometimes we don't see what's right in front of us because we're too focused on the important work we're doing—and often it's church work! Let's make sure we let Jesus have control of our calendar and our time-management bank account. I want to invest in the immeasurable abundant riches of Heaven. Don't you?

Great Sacrifice

We've all done something we are extremely ashamed of in our lifetime. Admit it. Maybe we never told another soul; in fact, we most likely desperately tried to forget. We cringe when a memory creeps back up, and we wish we could have a do-over. Unfortunately, we can't.

Guess what? That thing, that terrible sin, doesn't keep God from loving us! In fact, when Jesus was carrying His own cross to the place where He would die, He didn't rehearse our indiscretions and reconsider sacrificing Himself. No, it was the opposite. Jesus looked through the mist of time and saw me, and He saw you, knowing every bad choice we had made and would make in the future. Yet He was determined to pay the ultimate price to save His creation!

When we feel weighed down with the guilt and unforgiveness of the past, we have to open the Bible. There is no sin more powerful than the blood of Jesus Christ. When we feel unworthy of this loving sacrifice, we can read and be reminded that we did not make Him give up His life for us. Jesus willingly gave His life in exchange for ours.

"But God demonstrates His own love toward us, in that while we were still sinners, Christ died for us" (Romans 5:8). It's scandalous in its truth! Because of this great love gift, we are worthy to be called the children of God.

We can't go back and we don't need do-overs. Trying to hide from the hideous is needless. We live today in freedom from sin. "Looking unto Jesus, the author and finisher of our faith, who for the joy that was set before Him endured the cross, despising the shame, and has sat down at the right hand of the throne of God" (Hebrews 12:2).

We have a reason to rejoice today. God loves us and willingly died for us.

Hurricanes

Wind, rain, and storm-surging seas are a frequent occurrence on the Florida coast from May through November. We sit glued to our televisions, like the rest of the world, wondering, "What's going to happen?" For most residents, when the weather threatens disaster, the song "Should I Stay or Should I Go?" by The Clash plays in our heads.

When the wind kicks up in life, we're tempted to shake with fear too. We may panic and lose sight of the one who is ultimately in control. The twelve in the boat is a familiar Bible story. "The disciples went and woke Him, saying, 'Lord, save us! We're going to drown!' He replied, 'You of little faith, why are you so afraid?' Then He got up and rebuked the winds and the waves, and it was completely calm" (Matthew 8:25–26 NIV).

So often we ride the waves of anxiety when we worry about the trajectory of our future. I have experienced tragedy, and I know bad things happen. There's no trying to "figure it out." It's a matter of choice for me: I will trust the Sovereign Lord who loves me completely.

When my stomach starts to feel queasy and my nerves begin sizzling with fear, I lean into His Word. "The name of the LORD *is* a strong tower; The righteous run to it and are safe" (Proverbs 18:10). "But let all who take refuge in You be glad; let them ever sing for joy. Spread Your protection over them, that those who love Your name may rejoice in You" (Psalm 5:11 NIV).

Still, I sometimes waver, and I want to put my trust in my earthly capabilities and allow my finite mind to fret, "What is going to happen to me and the ones I love?" Even though the loving Savior has shown me time and again that His ways are perfect, I tend to want to believe my escape plan might be better.

With eyes glued on the storm, it's difficult to see anything else. We are creatures of survival; we fear disaster, and we want to live. Therefore we cry out, "Have mercy on me, my God, have mercy on me, for in You I take refuge. I will take refuge in the shadow of Your wings until the disaster has passed" (Psalm 57:1 NIV).

Turning our focus from the possibility of impending doom to Jesus, we'll likely discover that God has the best plan. He may not move the storm from our path, but only He can calm the "category five" in our hearts.

⸺ Backstory ⸺

We can learn a lot about people from their Facebook pages. Most of the time, it is simply the highlight reel, the parts of their lives they want to be seen. Sometimes, though, there is real insight if we stop to look closer.

I recently noticed a post from a mother who had lost her child to drowning several years ago. Her post pled, "If I have been unkind or short lately, please forgive me, I am just having a hard time dealing." This stayed with me throughout the day. I knew others who didn't know her or her situation may think she is quick-tempered. But by knowing people's stories, we are likely to be more understanding and extend more grace.

We come across people every day who may not be very pleasant or outgoing. They may need our smile, kindness, encouragement, and grace the most. We don't know what others are going through or what their backstories might be. When people are experiencing emotional or physical pain, it often affects the things they do and the way they act.

It's like the story of the woman at the well (John 4). With five previous husbands and a current live-in boyfriend, I'm certain she had a backstory. Did she have a father wound? Was she looking for love in all the wrong places? Jesus knew what she was struggling with and offered her everlasting love and "living water" (John 4:13–14).

Shouldn't we follow the example of Christ? Sometimes people might simply need to know someone cares, or they may need to hear the good news of the Living Water. We usually don't know people's backstory, but we know the one who can step into stories to mend broken hearts and heal wounds. Let's not keep Him to ourselves.

"Because of the Lord's great love, we are not consumed, for His compassions never fail" (Lamentations 3:22–23 NIV). God's mercy is new every morning, and He is faithful beyond our imaginations.

If we can recall the time Jesus walked into our stories and changed our lives forever, then we must pass it on.

Intentional Living

Not too long ago, I decided that I was going to get back to the gym. I already had a membership at a local fitness center, but a new spot opened that offered Pilates, yoga, and kickboxing. I joined that place too.

Three months later, I hadn't gone once. The problem? I was not being intentional about my health. A well-toned body wasn't going to magically happen. I had to start being deliberate about making wellness a priority.

We also must be intentional—do something on purpose—in our relationship with Christ. Activities important to our spiritual growth must be at the top of our list. Reading the Word, praying, telling the lost about Jesus, spending time with and encouraging other believers, and being the hands and feet of Christ enrich our relationship with the Savior.

Good intentions are great, but allowing other things to sneak up and take precedence is the downfall. There has to be action behind intent.

"Faith by itself, if it does not have works, is dead" (James 2:17). We must believe God and live a God-centered, Jesus-following life. When we see a person in need and have the ability to help, then we must take action.

> "For I was hungry and you gave Me food; I was thirsty and you gave Me drink; I was a stranger and you took me in; I was naked and you clothed Me, I was sick and you visited Me; I was in prison and you came to Me." Then the righteous will answer Him, saying "Lord, when did we see You hungry and feed You, or thirsty and give You drink? When did we see You a stranger and take You in, or naked and clothe You? Or when did we see You sick, or in prison and come to You?" And the King will answer and say to them, "Assuredly, I say to you, inasmuch as you did it to one of the least of these My brethren, you did it to Me." (Matthew 25:35–40)

When we see others through the eyes of Christ, we respond as He would.

Being a disciple of Jesus Christ is not always convenient, but it is always beneficial. If there is someone the Holy Spirit places on our hearts to reach out to, then we must give that person a call.

I tell myself, "Meredith, having a gym membership does not guarantee you a fit body. You must do something!" The same goes with being a Christian. Be intentional today. See, reach, give, tell, and love.

—— RIPPLE EFFECT ——

Each life creates a ripple effect. We are all connected by God's design, and He sees the entirety of every life past, present, and future. In my own heart, I believe God loves us so very much that He looks at circumstances that happen in this fallen world (illness, accidents, etc.) and says, "Right now is when bringing My child home will impact others for My glory and draw them to Me."

From the very beginning, the story of Joseph illustrates God's redeeming love. "You intended to harm me, but God intended it for good to accomplish what is now being done, the saving of many lives" (Genesis 50:20 NIV).

I once witnessed a family say goodbye to their sixteen-year-old son. I wept for their loss, and although I had only met Zach one time, he made an impression on me. He was engaging and kind; I could tell he was special. At the funeral, his mom shared his love for Jesus and others, and how Zach was not afraid to share his faith. Zach's family will never know on this side of eternity why Zach died so young.

Death is so deeply emotional and stunningly final. Since losing Mom to cancer and experiencing the sudden death of Lee, I have reconciled I will see them in Heaven and finally understand. I often remind myself that as children of God, our final destination is filled with awe and divine understanding, knowing all have been rescued.

My mom once was asked by a friend, "Jimi, why would God allow you to get cancer?"

After some thought, she answered, "Well, if one of my children, loved ones, or any lost soul grows closer or accepts Christ because of my journey, then it is worth it."

Her wisdom was gained through much study of the Scripture. In Acts 2, after Christ's death and resurrection, the day of Pentecost occurred, and thus began the Church. They worshiped together, struggled together, and took care of one another. They were willing to do whatever it took to spread the good news. "And the Lord added to their number daily those who were being saved" (Acts 2:47).

We are all witnesses to His saving grace, and we are called to be Jesus's hands and feet.

I believe if God had given Jimi, Lee, and Zachary a choice—a foreknowledge of their death and the ripple effect—each of them would have said, "Yes, Lord. The answer is yes!"

── HEAL US ──

One morning as I was reading my Bible, I swiftly read over the familiar instructions written by Paul. "Be anxious for nothing, but in everything by prayer and supplication, with thanksgiving, let your requests be made known to God; and the peace of God, which surpasses all understanding, will guard your hearts and minds through Christ Jesus" (Philippians 4:6–7).

I felt the Holy Spirit whisper, "Go back." I read the verse again, slowly this time. Breaking it down, I asked myself the hard question: "Do I do these things?" It had been a hard week, and I thought about all the times I had been stressed and worried. Ugh! I had failed miserably at "Be anxious for nothing." Trying to make myself feel better, I exhaled and said, "Well, Mer, you pray and you're thankful."

The next word, however, stopped me dead in my tracks. Supplication? Not a word I use often, if ever. I looked up the definition and read aloud. "The action of asking or begging for something earnestly or humbly." While I was growing up, our parents always told us not to beg, whine, or ask for something more than once. I figured it counted for God too.

Then I wondered if I'd been missing a very important ingredient in my prayer life. "Do I plead with God to show me His will? Do I earnestly pray for my children, friends, and community? Do I beg God to bring peace to our country? Do I kneel in humility, asking the heavenly Father what I can do to bring Him glory?" The answers made me sad.

I'm certain our world, our families, and our own fragile hearts would benefit from doing "everything by prayer and supplication." I know I long for "the peace of God, which surpasses all understanding."

This revelation to Scripture changed my approach to prayer. Unfortunately, there's no going back to change things, but starting with the present, I'm going to ask God to fill me with His love for others, heal all hearts, and free all His people from the bondage of fear. "If My people, who are called by My name, will humble themselves and pray and seek My face and turn from their wicked ways, then I will hear from heaven, and I will forgive their sin and will heal their land" (2 Chronicles 7:14).

Just imagine: "heal their land." In the midst of all the confusion, hatred, tragedy, and violence, this is a gloriously beautiful thought. Let us pray.

—— Predictably Unpredictable ——

I like routine. I love a good solid plan, and I'm ultra predictable. One Valentine's Day, Jon took me to one of our favorite restaurants. Our church had given all the married couples a date idea to order each other's meal. We decided to give it a try.

Jon will eat anything and usually orders something different each time we go out. I get the same exact meal every time at certain restaurants. On this date, when I ordered Jon's meal, I chose something I thought he would enjoy, and I expected him to order my usual. When he ordered something much different than my standard fare, I smiled politely, but my brain screamed, *What in the world? Why would he do that?*

Don't we do the same with God? We ask Him to intervene in our lives, and we invite Him to direct our paths. Yet when His plan deviates from what we expect, we balk.

As we waited for the food, I took a deep breath and said to myself, *I'm going to eat it no matter what,* even though I knew I wasn't going to like it. Do you know what? When my meal arrived and I tasted my first bite, I was surprised at how delicious it was! The food was cooked just right and instantly became a favorite.

We want what we want, but God knows what's best. "And my God will meet all your needs according to the riches of His glory in Christ Jesus" (Philippians 4:19). I still like predictability; I'm simply learning to be more flexible, to expand my outside-the-box thinking.

God is predictably unpredictable. He is trustworthy but doesn't always show up in the way we think He should. The Bible says, "For My thoughts are not your thoughts, nor are your ways My ways" (Isaiah 55:8).

The next time things don't go as planned, remember the saying, "When things seem to be falling apart, they may be falling into place."

One Easter weekend, Katy asked if she could read the resurrection story to Jon and me. We waited as she opened her Bible, and then we listened to her read about the empty tomb and the disciple's journey down the road to Emmaus.

"Mer, why didn't the disciples recognize Jesus? Didn't they know Him?" she stopped to ask.

I thought, *Oh, no! This is one of those teachable moments I'm pretty sure I'm going to blow!* I hesitantly answered, "Well, um, maybe it's because the last time they saw Jesus, He was beaten, bloody, and all scratched up, and now He is raised back to life and clean."

Her question stayed with me for a while. "Why didn't they recognize Jesus?" I read the account again, pouring over the Gospel of John, where Mary Magdalene is weeping at the tomb and encounters Jesus. She thought He was the gardener at first, but when He spoke her name, she instantly knew it was her Lord (John 20:11–18).

In Luke, the two disciples walking the road to Emmaus had seven miles with Jesus, and they also didn't know it was the Master. Later while eating together, they finally realized who had been with them the entire time (Luke 24:13–35). Surely they hit the heel of their hands to their foreheads, saying, "Duh, we should have known it was Him!"

I thought, *Wow. It took Mary less than five minutes to realize it was Jesus, and it took the men seven miles and dinner.* (Sorry, gentlemen.) While grieving the loss of their teacher and friend, they must have been distracted by their circumstances, momentarily forgetting all of the promises and prophecies Jesus had proclaimed. Instead of running to the tomb on the third day with total expectancy of His resurrection, they were surprised He had done exactly what He'd told them He would do.

I also thought, *I'm no better than they are!* We get so caught up in the thick of things, the disappointments and sorrows, that we fail to remember and claim God's sovereignty, provision, and redemption. On our darkest days, Jesus is right beside us.

I've heard it said all my life that the devil is in the details. That's only partly true. Satan is in the details of our blame, guilt, shame, and woeful wallowing. These are the distractions He uses to take our eyes off the Deliverer.

But Jesus cares about our every heartache and tear. He is there to greet us at the tomb and walk with us down the road. We must keep our eyes open to His presence, which is the gift of Easter. He died and rose in victory so that we can live with hope-filled expectancy.

── Two Buses ──

While living in a small town, I didn't get away with much as a teenager. And I didn't always appreciate it. As a parent, however, I usually knew what my kids were up to, and my appreciation of my tight-knit community grew.

The expression "It takes a village to raise a child" was proven true one high school prom season. Of the two buses rented to transport teens to the prom, one actually wasn't going to the prom. Parents spread the news, talked to one another, and encouraged their children to get on the "right" bus.

In life there also are two buses, and because God is a gentleman, He has given us the freedom to make a choice as to which one we board. He's also instructing us to make the right choice throughout His Word. "Enter by the narrow gate; for wide is the gate and broad is the way that leads to destruction, and there are many who go in by it. Because narrow is the gate and difficult is the way which leads to life, and there are few who find it" (Matthew 7:13–14).

My kids told me what seemed like a million times, "Mom, everybody else is doing it!" It certainly seems so, but the better way—though less popular and more difficult—actually leads to more freedom from sin, destruction, fear, and so much more. The path to abundant life appears to be the obvious choice. Yet the lure of instant, worldly gratification often skews our wisdom.

When standing at the crossroads, we must ask ourselves, "Will my choice glorify God, build my character, and lead others toward Christ?" If not, we'd be wise to go the other direction. Though the narrow way may look lonely at first, on this journey, "There is a friend who sticks closer than a brother" (Proverbs 18:24). And He is with us always, "even to the end of the age" (Matthew 28:20).

Jesus offers so much more than temporary pleasure. He wants to gift us with abundance and freedom. Climb aboard the bus that will get you safely home.

——— Words ———

"My darling, hateful words are like bullets: once they are released, you can't take them back. And when they hit their mark, they always leave a scar." That's how Momma answered my fourteen-year-old question about why someone in our family was getting a divorce. She knew it wasn't appropriate for me to hear the details of the adult situation at the time, but she wanted me to know how powerful words are.

It was the first and only time my mom gave me such advice. However, it made an impact then, and over the next thirty or so years, the lesson has come to mind time and again.

Scripture says, "Death and life are in the power of the tongue" (Proverbs 18:21). Also, "The words of the reckless pierce like swords, but the tongue of the wise brings healing" (Proverbs 12:18 NIV). James, the half-brother of Jesus, says, "No man can tame the tongue. It is a restless evil, full of deadly poison" (James 3:8).

That's powerful teaching! So, how can we keep from speaking ugly words to one another? God gave us the solution when, through Paul, Scripture tells us, "Casting down every argument and every high thing that exalts itself against the knowledge of God, bringing every though into captivity to the obedience of Christ" (2 Corinthians 10:5). And then there's "Whatever things are true, whatever things are noble, whatever things are just, whatever things are pure, whatever things are lovely, whatever things are of good report, if there is any virtue and if there is anything praiseworthy—meditate on these things." (Philippians 4:8).

Christ is the only way to bring our wayward minds and mouth muscles into submission. Hurtful thoughts and words toward others are careless and often rooted deep inside. "For the mouth speaks what the heart is full of" (Luke 6:45 NIV). My mom used to say, "Garbage in, garbage out."

Let's pray for our hearts, thoughts, and words every morning before we even greet our family, co-workers, and friends. We can fill our hearts and minds with the good things of God by reading His word and remembering to encourage others with words that affirm and lift. When Christ is in the forefront of our hearts and minds, we don't spew hateful words but only speak love.

—— Dream ——

My family members and close friends know I dream frequently. I don't share my dreams with many people, but one a few years ago left a big impression.

I dreamed I was on an airplane and trying to sleep. People around me were shouting that the plane was going down and we were going to crash. I lifted my head and calmly told those around me, "Don't worry; it won't hurt when we hit the ground. But you want to make sure you have a relationship with Jesus. It's not too late."

Then I woke up. I remember wondering how many of the two hundred or more passengers knew Him as the Way, the Truth, and the Life.

It's scary to tell people they need a Savior, but God always opens the door for us to share our faith. He also gives us the courage. Sometimes we don't even have to say a word; our faith can shine on good days and even on days full of trial. My mom used to tell me, "Sweetheart, your life may be the only Bible someone will ever read, so let them see Jesus in your day-to-day walk, and they will want what you have."

Some days we can feel like we're on a collision course with anxiety and devastation. When fear presses in, speak the words of David: "Whenever I am afraid, I will trust in You" (Psalm 56:3). Faith dissolves fear, much like the sun burns away the morning mist.

The day will come when we'll each face the Creator and Judge. Will we be found faithful? Now, while we're still living, do we ask ourselves, "Am I sharing the good news of salvation or keeping it to myself?"

It's never too late to surrender our souls to Christ, no matter who we are and what we've done. The heavenly Pilot is waiting to welcome everyone to first class.

— WHO ARE YOU? —

Imagine meeting someone for the first time. A conversation begins, and before long the question pops up: "So, what do you do for a living?" Once the question is answered, this is likely how you are defined in each other's minds: banker, doctor, homemaker, construction supervisor, outside sales, teacher, pastor.

We subconsciously give ourselves titles. I am a widow, divorcee, orphan; I am unworthy, unloved, unclean, a failure. We think who we are consists of the roles we play or the things that have happened to us. But the labels we put on ourselves are not what God calls us.

God's Word is the ultimate truth, so let's look and see what it says about who we are. How we are defined by God is much different than how we sometimes define ourselves or how the world might define us.

We are God's "sons and daughters" (2 Corinthians 6:18), His "friend" (John 15:15), and God's "masterpiece" (Ephesians 2:10). We are "altogether beautiful" (Song of Solomon 4:7). My very favorite is that we are His "beloved" (Song of Solomon 6:3).

Are we going to believe the Word or the world? When Satan's lies invade our minds and we think of ourselves as less than lovely, we must not let the evil one's belittling take up space in our heads.

One of the hardest things for us to comprehend is the unconditional love of Christ. We are very hard on ourselves. And the rest of the world? Let's just say it can be ruthless. If Satan can't destroy us, he will try to distract us and tear us down with untruths.

Here's the challenge. Write down on one sheet of paper who we "think" we are, and on another write who God says we are. Now, burn the first piece, because who God says we are is the only thing that matters.

Be encouraged. He sees us through the precious blood of His only Son, and we are His beautiful and beloved children.

───── CHOOSE THE GOOD PART ─────

I rarely cook dinner. My mother-in-law cooks for the entire family every weekday evening. Yes, I am a blessed woman. This generous woman takes a task off my plate (pun intended) after a long workday and allows us to sit down together for a family meal. Plus, I actually love spending time with my in-laws.

One night as we finished eating and began to talk, I started gathering the plates. (The least I can do is wash the dishes!) Mimi suggested, "Why don't you sit and relax some more?"

I realized in that moment that I am a woman of action. I'm accustomed to finishing a task at work and then going directly to the next file, phone call, or crisis; I have programmed myself to keep moving. This developed trait was keeping me from relaxing and enjoying the moment. Past experience has taught me that the people we love and cherish may not be with us forever, yet I was missing out on creating memories.

This is reminiscent of another woman named Martha. She too was missing out on some really good stuff. In the Gospel of Luke, Martha and her sister, Mary, were hosts to Jesus and His disciples. Mary sat at the feet of Jesus and soaked up His every word while Martha was in the kitchen, focused on getting the meal prepared. When Martha complained about doing all the work, Jesus enlightened her. "Martha, Martha, you are worried and troubled about many things. But one thing is needed, and Mary has chosen that good part, which will not be taken away from her" (Luke 10:41–42).

Jesus knew He would not be with His friends for much longer, and while Mary was soaking up His wisdom and creating memories, Martha thought she was doing what "needed" to be done. In reality, the dishes would always be there to wash, and someone would always be there for her to serve. However, this special moment with Jesus would not always be there.

There are appropriate times for action, as well as times for being still and listening. Constant busyness, running from one task to the next, may cost precious moments and missed memories. Remember that distractions often destroy.

Sitting in the Word, communing with God, and carving out memories with loved ones are priceless.

—— Follow or Not ——

When I was on a work trip once with Jon in Starkville, Mississippi, we were invited to dinner at the home of one of his old teammates, who became the head baseball coach for Mississippi State University. Jon and I both are directionally challenged, and so we used our GPS most of the trip. The Cohens live about fifteen miles on the outskirts of town, but we arrived without getting lost.

Heading back to the hotel was another story. It was dark and rainy, and there were tornado warnings in the area. We turned the wrong way upon leaving the neighborhood. A few miles later, we decided to put the hotel address into the GPS. Next thing we knew, the nice lady told us to turn down what we quickly realized was a dirt road. It narrowed dangerously, and we talked about turning around. However, with the rain, mud, and deep ditches on each side, that wasn't possible. We drove slowly forward. When we came to a rickety bridge, I was skeptical as we crossed, but we made it. Phew! Once it was practical to turn around, we had to decide: do we turn off the GPS and navigate ourselves, or do we keep following the voice?

I thought about Solomon's wise words. "But the path of the just is like the shining sun, that shines ever brighter unto the perfect day" (Proverbs 4:18). I prayed for some light. We didn't know what was ahead of us, and our surroundings looked a lot like a scene from the movie *Deliverance*. Utterly lost, with the rain pounding on the windshield, we dreaded the thought that the GPS was wrong. I felt a moment of panic; a trickle of fear ran down my spine.

We pushed ahead, deciding to follow the GPS, and made it safely to our hotel. My blood pressure finally returned to normal. I thought to myself, *That detour was a lot like life.*

We certainly don't know what's ahead. Hopefully it's easy travels, but most likely it's also detours, potholes, and dead ends. We will reach our final destination easier if we read the map (God's Word), trust Jesus's promises, and follow the leading of the Holy Spirit. "In all your ways acknowledge Him, and He shall direct your paths" (Proverbs 3:6).

Don't turn off the GPS: God's Plan of Salvation. Lay fears at the feet of the One who knows the path perfectly, and grow closer to Him while on the journey.

"I am the way, the truth, and the life. No one comes to the Father except through Me" (John 14:6). Jesus is the ultimate GPS, and following Him always leads to home.

——— WILDFIRES ———

Dry conditions from seasonal drought, along with high winds, have destroyed thousands of acres in Florida, wreaking havoc on crops, homes, and lives. Fires can begin with a tiny spark or a controlled burn that gets out of control. The person innocently burning backyard trash or leaving a still-smoldering campfire unattended probably doesn't think about the potential for widespread harm.

Much like devastating wildfires, when our souls are parched due to lack of "water" (communion with God and reading His Word), we are more susceptible to sin. What we think of as small and harmless could become a roaring fire of destruction in our lives. Fortunately, the Creator knows us so well that He lovingly warns of the things He knows can hinder our relationship with Him and others.

James 3 reminds us that the tongue, while purposed for good (speaking, in this example), has the ability to cause tremendous pain to others, as well as lie. "It corrupts the whole body, sets the whole course of one's life on fire" (James 3:6 NIV). The eyes too can get us into trouble. Jesus gives the example, "But I tell you that anyone who looks at a woman lustfully has already committed adultery with her in his heart" (Matthew 5:28 NIV).

God's fire safety manual, the Bible, doesn't exaggerate. He knows us better than we know ourselves. In our world, think about the little white lie, the flirty glance, or the "just one drink" promise, and then recall the careers, marriages, and years of sobriety that have been wrecked. Of course, Satan wants us to believe a "little sin" is harmless." But Scripture sets us straight. Jesus says, "The thief does not come except to steal, and to kill, and to destroy. I have come that they may have life, and that they may have it more abundantly" (John 10:10).

Although what starts out as small may not seem so bad, it can expand and enslave or trap us without warning. God wants us to live in the freedom of His grace. "Jesus answered them, 'Most assuredly, I say to you, whoever commits sin is a slave of sin. And a slave does not abide in the house forever, but a son abides forever. Therefore, if the Son makes you free, you shall be free indeed'" (John 8:34–36).

Be quick to recognize a spark of sin that could turn into a wildfire. Act quickly and reach for the extinguisher; open the Bible, and turn to the ultimate Savior. Jesus drenches the soul with His love and forgiveness, and spiritual drought becomes only a distant memory.

─── God Revealed in Us ───

We wonder why bad things happen to good people. Even though we know God allows the natural consequences of our choices to unfold, often it's easy to feel like He's angry. The *why* comes in when we're living in a right relationship with Him and bad stuff happens.

There's a Bible story about a man who was blind since birth. Jesus's disciples saw the man and asked, "'Rabbi, who sinned, this man or his parents, that he was born blind?' Jesus answered, 'Neither this man nor his parents sinned, but that the works of God should be revealed in him'" (John 9:2–3). There have been times I've had similar questions. "What did I do to deserve this, God?" The Scripture in John teaches this is backward thinking. God sometimes allows situations so that He can be glorified. Doing the work of His Father, Jesus restores the blind man's sight, and many witnesses were awed.

We often look inward at our own situation or debilitation, not understanding why things are the way they are. From a small inconvenience to a terrible tragedy, it's very easy to forget life isn't all about us. We certainly may not have caused or deserve the challenges we face, but we are part of a bigger story—God's story.

Remember that we have a secure heritage and are assured earthly suffering is not in vain. "The Spirit Himself testifies with our spirit that we are God's children. Now if we are children, then we are heirs—heirs of God and co-heirs with Christ, if indeed we share in His sufferings in order that we may also share in His glory. I consider that our present sufferings are not worth comparing with the glory that will be revealed in us" (Romans 8:16–18 NIV).

Pain and misery are difficult. Yet, if we can grasp the truth that God never forsakes us but uses circumstances for the greater good of building His eternal kingdom, then the suffering may ease a bit. Joy may seem far right away now and trusting God's plan too hard, but His love is faithful. He will carry you until you feel strong enough to walk again and can proclaim, "To God be the glory."

——— Ready and Willing ———

The Bible story about the little boy with five loaves of bread and two small fish (John 6) is a good reminder our Lord is a miracle worker. But think about it: What if the boy had said, "I can't give you my food because it may not be good enough," and, "I may not have enough for myself." What if he was so worried about what other people might think of his gift that he hid it?

We know Jesus could have spoken an ample supply of food into existence. However, He wanted the boy to be a part of glorifying the Provider.

> He said, "Bring them here to Me." Then He commanded
> the multitudes to sit down on the grass. And He took the
> five loaves and the two fish, and looking up to heaven,
> He blessed and broke and gave the loaves to the disciples;
> and the disciples gave to the multitudes. So they all ate
> and were filled, and they took up twelve baskets full of
> the fragments that remained. (Matthew 14:18–20)

The boy's willingness to share what he had not only exalted Jesus right then and there but also lasted for generations to come. Imagine him telling his family and friends about his firsthand encounter with the Savior of the world. What an impact one child's selflessness had on the kingdom.

What are we holding back that could be used to glorify God and further His work? And *why* do we hold it back? What lie do we believe? That we'll be laughed at, be called a failure, or be rejected? Are we worried our ugly past eliminates us from serving Him?

The truth is that if our gift is time, talent, money, or resources, God will use it for His glory. Whatever is offered with an obedient and willing heart pleases Him, no matter how small or insignificant we may think it is. And just as Jesus told the disciples to gather up the remaining pieces of food, He has a plan for the leftovers in our lives. With Christ, nothing is wasted!

If we are willing, He will use us and our gifts, and He will not leave us, or our hands, empty. We are worthy, and we are useful. God is waiting to have it all.

—— Amazing Grace ——

One Sunday morning, my pastor opened with the question, "Is the amazing grace you experienced at the time of salvation still amazing to you?" It caught my attention, and I must admit I didn't hear much of his message after that. My thoughts were hijacked by how unfathomable it is that God's love for us is so great He would sacrifice His only Son for sinful mankind.

Scripture proclaims, "For God so loved the world that He gave His only begotten Son, that whoever believes in Him should not perish but have everlasting life" (John 3:16). When we forget the details of that sacrifice, our feelings of gratitude may wane, but it doesn't lessen the magnitude of the sacrifice.

Remember falling in love? The fast heart beats and wide smiles, with every thought and sighting of that person. The elation of being together. But as time went by and the relationship grew more comfortable, even though the frequent feelings of euphoria may have waned, the love didn't.

What about God's grace? New believers are often on fire and overwhelmed with the realization of Jesus's death and resurrection. As time goes by and spiritual maturity grows, the gratitude may grow complacent unless His grace and sacrifice are front and center. The brutal scenes from *The Passion of the Christ* evoke an emotional reaction, quicken our memories, and take us back to the moment we accepted Christ as Savior.

As a young person, I heard a story about an orphan boy who was adopted by a king. He was given new clothes and a steward of his own. Every morning, the steward watched as the boy dragged a box from behind his bedroom door, stood in front of the mirror, held in front of him the rags he used to wear, and cry. After several months, the steward finally asked the boy, "Why do you keep those ragged clothes in a box, and why do you hold them up in the mirror and cry?"

With tears in his eyes and a smile on his face, the boy said, "I never want to forget what the king did for me!"

We too have been adopted and redeemed. And though we do not need to rehearse our sin, we certainly should reminisce often that moment of the beautiful exchange when we surrendered to the Savior, and He took our sins and in turn extended His grace.

My Deepest Thanks

When I first felt an early tug in my heart to write this book, I resisted. The thought of being vulnerable back in 2015 didn't appeal to me, and the dread of reliving my grief loomed heavy. But through sharing bits and pieces of my story on Facebook with my sunrise photos, I discovered the world is full of hurting people who desire encouragement and hope.

I was also hesitant to put a spotlight on my story and the devastating death of Lee, because I worried it would overshadow the wonderful love I now share with Jon. But Jon urged me to believe that my story (in book form) is also part of God's plan, and to trust the divine timing and purpose of us.

My incredible husband is my biggest fan, and I could not ask for a more perfect life mate with whom to serve the Lord and walk through the midlife and senior years together. Thank you, Jon, for your all-in, amazing heart and the delight you bring to my life every single day.

As I prayed God's guidance, the words began to flow. I shared the pages with my daughter, Jimi, who was my partner in prayer over this project and my number one source of encouragement. As I sent Jimi the raw pieces of myself on paper, she lovingly returned honest and useful feedback. My other prayer warrior and book confidante was my mother-in-law, Joyce Shave, also known as Mimi. She was brutally forthright with her opinions (which I secretly love), and she never failed to offer support. Mimi called me often on Saturday mornings to ask, "Well, are you writing? You'd better get busy!"

I am so thankful for Jimi's soul-deep belief in me and Joyce's mothering love and cheerleading. Without these two faith-filled women and their constant validation, I'm not sure I would have been brave enough to keep on writing.

A window opened for me in September 2017 in a way other people might think was a door closing. I was given the opportunity to talk with a well-known Christian author and was excited to glean knowledge and guidance from her. She encouraged me to attend a writer's conference and offered some tips. Then she broke the news that my manuscript would most likely never get published traditionally. She shared that if I wasn't a known author, famous, or bizarre (like Octomom), no one would likely want to read my story. She was honest, and I was discouraged.

But God used that experience for good. That conversation prompted me to search the Internet for a Christian book coach, and I found Lee McCracken. Her tender heart and mine immediately melded. What a gift she is. God knew exactly who I needed to help me to the finish line. Thank you, Lee, for being not only a talented writer, editor, and coach but also a dear sister in Christ. Your heart for the things of God and others is inspiring.

I also want to thank Angie for proving that distance does not limit friendship. Ben, thank you for all of the advice over the years, and for being like a brother. Beth, you know everything about me and still love me, which is truly a gift. Bianca, my sixth sister, you encourage me daily, I am blessed to have you in my life. "RA!" Kara, your friendship, godly wisdom, and faithfulness inspire me to do likewise. Lindsay (Lou), "shame friend," you are one of a kind, and I love you. Lynn: wow, just wow; I would have to write another book to express how God has used you in my life. Thank you for being sensitive to His promptings; it changed our lives forever. Pam, your friendship and 6:00 a.m. Friday Starbucks dates are a highlight of my week. Tiffany, thank you for listening to me for hours upon hours of treadmill talk; you are wise beyond your years. Christy (you should have been a truck driver) and Laura, thank you for driving me to meet my book coach, because without you two, I probably would have ended up in Miami instead of North Carolina.

Dr. Linda and Dr. Judy, I can never thank you enough for your wisdom, love, and counsel. Thank you, Claudia (my soul sister) and George, for welcoming me into your home, giving me time to regroup and begin healing. Carolyn and Todd, thank you for making me leave my house and go to dinners with you (even if you did threaten to make me go in my pajamas if not dressed in ten minutes); you two never forgot about me. To the many others who encouraged, inspired, and loved me along the way: thank you.

When I think back over the years, my testimony of Jesus's saving grace in the midst of any storm is out of the fullness of joy I feel today. Thank you for reading my story and opening your heart to healing. May the Holy Spirit flood your soul with His peace.

Love,
Mer

About the Author

Meredith Shave is a wife, mother and grandmother who lives the hope of Jesus with every sunrise on her beloved Florida First Coast. With more than 20 years in the mortgage industry, she nurtures her creative side by writing and taking photographs at the beach. She also has a deep love of horses and finds joy in riding. Meredith was raised in the church and sang with her families performing group throughout her childhood. Her life's story is a testimony to God's redeeming grace.